Surviving the
Forgotten Armenian Genocide
A moving personal story

Surviving the
Forgotten Armenian Genocide
A moving personal story

Smpat Chorbadjian

Edited by Patrick Sookhdeo

Isaac Publishing

Surviving the Forgotten Armenian Genocide:
A moving personal story
© 2015 Isaac Publishing

Published in the United States by
Isaac Publishing, 6729 Curran Street, McLean VA 22101

Library of Congress Control Number: 2015937347

ISBN: 978-0-9916145-7-8

Book design by Lee Lewis Walsh, Words Plus Design

Printed in the United States of America

Contents

Foreword

As I travel around the world, I have the privilege of meeting Christians from all backgrounds and nationalities. It is always a joy to meet Armenians, who have been scattered across the globe because of persecution, like the early Christians (Acts 8:1), and have settled wholeheartedly into their new contexts (Jeremiah 29:4-7). But every Armenian family I have ever met carries a sorrow that has burdened them for a hundred years – the tragedy of the lost generation who suffered and died in what Armenians call their "Golgotha".

The year 1915 was the pivotal one in almost three decades of violence inflicted on the Armenian inhabitants of the Ottoman Empire. Because of the vast scale and centrally planned strategy of the killings, most historians agree that this was genocide.

This book is the frank and candid story of one survivor of the Armenian genocide, Smpat Chorbadjian. There is much to shock the reader, not only the brutal suffering inflicted on the Armenians, but also the desperate measures required to survive it, not all of which are recorded here. For example, the family recalls that when Smpat's father died he was sad, but when his mother died he was relieved because it had been such a responsibility to care for her. He immediately cut up the sheet she had been lying on and sold it as headscarves for Muslim women.

But any Armenian will tell you a similar story of their own grandparents or great-grandparents.

Surviving the Forgotten Armenian Genocide: a Moving Personal Story is a tale of two journeys. We travel with Smpat around the Middle East, in the tumultuous years of the early 20th century and through the unspeakable horrors he witnesses and endures. But it is not until the final pages that Smpat reveals his journey of faith. As an Armenian, Smpat was born into a strong Christian heritage, which was very precious to him. But a life-changing personal encounter with Jesus Christ on 6 February 1931 opened for him a new dimension of trusting God and walking with Him.

After the tempestuous events of this narrative, Smpat spent the rest of his life peacefully in Cyprus. He worked as a tailor in Nicosia and brought up his three sons, the eldest of whom, Sam, joined him in business and went into the clothing trade. When Sam was advised by an English customer to move to Limassol because all the English were settling there, Sam duly went to reconnoitre the possibilities. In those days it was a two-hour drive on narrow roads from Nicosia. On arrival, he strolled around the town and spotted an empty shop in St Andrew's Street, enquired for the owner, contacted him, and made a deal with him to rent the premises. Sam and his wife moved to Limassol and the following year, 1961, Smpat joined them. The other two sons also moved to Limassol so the whole family was united there. After a period of poor health, Smpat died on 11 April 1963.

I am very grateful to Smpat's sons and their wives for allowing us to make known his story. This version has been translated from the original, which was written in Turkish language but employing

Armenian script. The stark simplicity of the narrative has been retained in order to preserve the authenticity of Smpat's voice.

I pray that this moving testimony of survival and faith will be an inspiration to many.

Patrick Sookhdeo PhD, DD
March 2015

Preface

It has been pressing on my heart to write the history of my life. This is a story of things I have seen and experienced. I started to write this on 18 February 1941, from memory. I hope my readers will not expect exact dates and times. In fact you will discover when reading this that not only can I not remember days and months; it can be challenging now for me to remember what day of the week it is! I can only assure you that there is no lie, no exaggeration and no addition to my actual experiences. I have written what I remember, and what I have written is the truth.

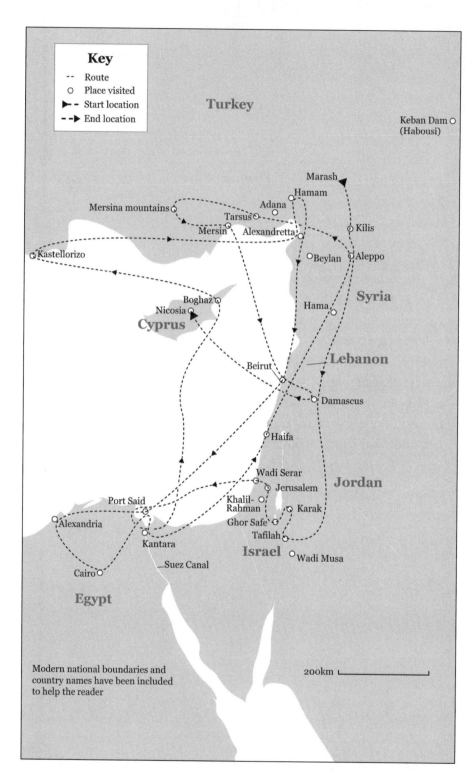

Smpat Chorbadjian's Journeys

Chapter 1

Forced to Leave

I Begin My Life Story

To start my story I first need to establish my birth date, as my birth certificate was lost. In 1895, the Turks came to Marash [today called Kahramanmaras] and slaughtered a huge Armenian population there. According to my mother, I was born three years after this massacre, which would set my birthdate at 1898.

I was born in Marash, now part of Turkey, in the house of Haroutune Agha Chorbadjian. As I grew up and began to discern good and evil, I realised that I was the son of a good, happy family. I had a father, mother, brothers and sisters, and although my father was not rich, we were comfortable. We had a vineyard in the best resort of the town, where we would spend the summer months. I had three sisters, all married. Then tragedy struck. My eldest sister's husband died, leaving his young widow to care for two small children. Soon afterwards, both my younger sisters died, by the will of God. I was already a schoolboy at that time. I had an older brother, Yervant, and two younger brothers, Timoteos and Sarkis.

Then in 1909 large-scale Armenian massacres started again in Adana, Turkey, and spread to many places. They came to Marash, too, but the governor at that time, Moukhtasar Moutessarif, did not go along with the plans. One Saturday morning when the killing was to have taken place, they attacked, running through the streets with axes and knives, killing any who were found on the streets or in the shops. It lasted about 15 minutes and 50-60 Armenians were killed. I was eleven years old at the time. We had a small powder gun in the house for scaring people; it could not fire cartridges. I took the dummy gun and rushed into the street to kill the Turks. My mother and sisters were in the market at that time and I wanted to save them. When my mother saw me, she took the gun away by force. The killing did not last long, and soon my father and brother also arrived safely home. We all got back to work, and life returned to normal.

Until 1914, all was well. I had finished preparatory school and became apprentice to a tailor, but once the war started, I could no longer continue this. The government started collecting a number of different taxes from each home. Another massacre was also planned in Marash, but instead they began deporting families, forcing them from their homes and sending them to remote countries. In 1915 the Armenian deportation began.

There was an Armenian village near Marash called Zeytoun. The brave men of this village had been resisting the Turkish government and from time to time had led certain uprisings in the defence of the Armenians. Many times they had fought government troops and come out victorious. No massacre had ever succeeded in their village. But in 1915 the Armenian situation was so delicate and critical that the nation begged this village to surrender themselves for the sake of the Armenians in other Turkish provinces whose lives were also in danger. The Zeytoun villagers agreed to the request, and surrendered to the Turkish government on condition that they would be allowed to come and live in Marash.

The brave leader of the Zeytoun village, Sergeant Nazareth, was brought to the Marash prison, where he "died" after a few days.

After his death, the other villagers began to arrive. Some were put up in the inn; others were sent out of town into the surrounding fields. It was winter time. The weather was cold and wet. We Armenians in Marash tried to help them by taking food and warm clothing out to them, but the government would not allow us to do this. The "prisoners" were kept guarded by *jandarmas* (Turkish soldiers). Sometimes we managed to smuggle some wood to them by bribing the guards, but the ground was so wet it was difficult to start a fire in the open field. Then they were ordered to march. Old and young, women and children, all began to walk to their unknown destination.

Now it was the turn of the other villages around Marash. Deportees arrived in our town in a miserable condition. One village, Findijak, resisted the deportation order. When troops came to take them by force, the villagers turned and fought, even managing to kill many Turkish soldiers in the fight. Then the people of the village divided into two parties. One party hoisted the white flag and surrendered, while the other party escaped to the mountains, where they resisted the Turks until the end of the war. The party who had surrendered were brought to Marash in a terrible condition, barefoot and wounded. Soon they too were deported from Marash, to perish from cold and hunger on the road.

The Deportation of Armenians from Marash

Finally, our turn came. First, all the prominent Armenians in Marash were ordered to leave. They were to make for Aleppo, and stay there. Twelve families left, although not all made it to Aleppo. Some were taken to the Der el Zor desert, where thousands of Armenians were massacred during the war. Then a new order came for all men between 18 and 45. They had 24 hours to leave their homes. They were to take one blanket and some food and gather in a field outside Marash. My elder brother, Yervant, was among them.

By this time, people were willing to be deported. Any method of getting away from Marash was welcomed. Every morning we would hear that five or ten people had been hanged that night. We would wake up to the sounds of crying and mourning from every house. During the day, more people would be shot and dumped in a big limestone pit, so the sound of weeping and mourning never stopped, day or night, from every house. It was better to die en route than to be hanged, shot, or cruelly tortured in your own house. At that time we received a letter from my brother Yervant, saying he was well, and was staying at Hama, Syria, at a place near the railway station.

In 1915 an order came to everyone in the Kumbet district to be ready and waiting in a field outside of town, to be deported. I was quite grown up by now. The government did us a great and unexpected kindness by allowing each family a donkey to load their belongings on to. My father managed to hire two extra donkeys, and we packed food, clothing, and some bedding on to these. We could take nothing else. We wanted to sell some of our household belongings, but no-one would buy Armenian goods. They all knew that soon enough the Armenians would be deported and they could help themselves to anything they wanted! So we left our house and everything in it and began to walk away, weeping as we went.

Our family and my uncle's family together, about 18 of us from one house, gathered in the field known as Marash Alti, "Below Marash". From there we went to Kara-Biyikli, "The Black Moustache", where we spent the night. The villagers in this area were desperate characters, cut-throats and robbers. We, of course, were on foot, and if anyone remained a little behind the villagers caught them and killed them. All that night long the menfolk kept watch, together with the two *jandarma* who were guarding us.

Early the next morning we resumed our walk and in the late evening we reached the town of Aintab. All communication with the town was forbidden; we were not even allowed to go in and buy some essentials. Again, the following morning from crack of dawn till evening we continued walking, women, children and elderly; all our feet were beginning to swell and cause much pain. Some of the ladies were not even used to working in their own homes. They had had several servants working for them. Even the young men were not used to this much walking. Now, the cruel whips in the *jandarmas'* hands encouraged them to keep walking. At last, we arrived at a town called Kilis.

In Kilis we met some people from Gurun. They were refugees like us. They had been walking for about a month, wandering from one place to another. There was no male older than 13 among their group. They had separated the men and massacred them on the way. The women and young girls continued; their legs and feet were bleeding, swollen and covered in sores. Still, the *jandarmas'* whips obliged them to keep walking. Those who fell on the way never got up again. Many had already died. Those who survived joined our group, and we walked together from Kilis toward Katma. One woman had a son who was very sick. Soon he was no longer able to walk. I saw the woman take the child and hide him under a bush, in the shade. Then she began to walk away, continually looking behind her, weeping. As she was walking, looking behind her, weeping, a *jandarma* rushed on her and began to whip her. I could watch no more. He was still whipping her when I ran away, into the group of walkers. Finally, we reached Katma.

Katma

Katma was a large railway station, the centre for deportations. Armenian refugees were brought here and from here they were sent away to be massacred. We waited in Katma for about eight days. Sometimes the villagers brought some food to us, but they sold it at very high prices. Every night the men would keep watch, guarding our few belongings. There were policemen there, but they were not much interested in guarding the Armenians' belongings from the robbers!

There were thousands of Armenians in Katma waiting to be deported. Everywhere families were huddled under their blankets or pieces of sack, which made a shelter from the heat of the sun. Then our turn came. We were loaded into a goods wagon and at night we reached Aleppo. The train stopped here, and Bedros, a young lad that I knew personally, came down to find some water. The policemen caught him and beat him up so much he barely managed to throw himself back into the wagon. That same night we left Aleppo and reached Hama. Just before dawn, hearing that we had arrived, my brother and some young men hid in one of the wagons, and then came and joined us.

Next, we arrived at Damascus, where we changed trains, to the Hiyaz railway line. We travelled some distance from Damascus and were approaching a station called Jouroufun Dervish when the train stopped. The wood for the engine had run out, we were told. During the war, Turkey had run out of coal. At this very moment thousands of Armenians were, therefore, working in the forests cutting wood to further Turkey's war effort. Young men were preferred for this job. The Turkish government killed their wives and children in front of them, but they were generously spared to labour in the forests and build roads for the Turks. When the mission was accomplished they were sent to join their wives.

We came off the train and began gathering twigs and thorns for the engine. Thus we finally reached Jouroufun Dervish, where we stayed, camped out in a field near the station, sheltering under our blankets from the terrible heat of that place. We stayed there for about three days. The most terrible thing was that they locked the water tank and no water was given at all. There was a little water to be bought, but at terrible prices. We had no water with us at all. We managed to take a little from the soldiers, but in the terrible hot weather this was nowhere near enough. It was maddening to think of the lovely, large supply in the tank, when we were not allowed any. The next day a group of us took our water skins and escaped in search of water. A little down the path we found a well. It was very deep, but there were iron steps down the side. My brother Timoteos went down and fetched up some water. I went next and filled my water skin. Then the Turks found us. From that day there was a soldier put to guard this well and make sure the Armenians didn't get any water from it.

Three days later we woke up to see many Arabs had joined our party. On their heads were the typical Arab *agils*, with long locks of black hair and long white shirts that reached the ground, and black *meshlah* cloaks. They were barefooted; the soles of their feet were so thick they reminded you of camels' hooves. Each one had an English rifle on his shoulder and about 100 cartridges, donkeys' reins and saddles, all strange looking to us. We had never seen anything like it before and were much afraid. They stayed there that day and the next day transportations began. They were taking us to Tafilah, a small town ruled by a *kaymakam*, or governor. Tafilah was a good place, we were told. Those who bribed the transport officer would be taken to Tafilah. Everyone else would be sent to the villages. We gave them some money, and we were given donkeys for the transportation. Then we were set on our way. Timoteos was suffering badly from sore eyes at the time. We travelled hard all day and at night we arrived at Tafilah.

Chapter 2

The Hardships of Daily Life

Now We Are at Tafilah

When we reached Tafilah we were taken to an old castle. There were no windows to let any sunshine in, and the place was terribly damp and smelly. We stayed there a few days, and every day our numbers increased as more and more refugees arrived. My uncle was taken to a village called Sunfiye, three miles away. We were separated from him at the station. We lived instead with a close friend of my father's. The "houses" where they were living were four walls and a makeshift roof covering them, and an earthen floor. It was little better than the castle, but at least we were away from the lice! My brother was still suffering from sore eyes. We found a woman who could make up medicines, but she couldn't find the medicine we needed for him.

Lice started troubling us badly. The more we washed them away, the more they seemed to multiply! As if that wasn't enough, we had a problem with fleas in our house too. One day in the summer time we were sleeping on the roof of the house. Our landlord had found a key to our door, and he broke in during the night. Every bit of clothing or anything else that was any good at all he took. There was even a little money among the clothes. We reported the incident to the government and they found the thief, but they could do nothing about it because the whole village was rebellious against the government.

My brother's eyes became increasingly worse. Where exactly did one find an eye specialist in this god-forsaken place anyway? Instead, we took him to the government doctor, and he gave him some medicine. For a couple of days he seemed to do better, and the doctor changed the medicine. After that his eyes swelled up completely and for one month he couldn't open them at all. When he finally did, we saw that there were wounds in his eyes each bigger than a grain of lentil. Naturally, these were causing him terrible pain. One eye was virtually blind, the other only a little better. By this time the lice had been on a rampage, and typhoid was spreading like wildfire among the refugees.

As the typhoid spread, causing misery in each house, it opened the floodgates to other infections and diseases. Every house could boast of two or three critically ill patients. In our house my father's friend died, then his wife. His son, daughter and daughter-in-law moved to another house. The same day we received the news that my uncle also had died. Two days later his eldest son died, leaving a young widow and three children. We were sick too. My father sent word for my cousin Baroyr to come and stay with us. He was a clever young man of about twenty-five, a teacher by profession. My father was very fond of him. He came as soon as he received our message, but the priest, Father Krikor, who was a relative of ours, asked if Baroyr could stay with him to help. Every week he led a church service, and Baroyr would help him in this. Typhoid struck there too, and the priest died, and Baroyr was bedridden. Next we heard that Baroyr's mother had died, and the next day my cousin Khoren died. None of this did we tell to Baroyr. In the end, all four brothers and the father and mother died, leaving only the daughter-in-law alive in that family, with the three children. Baroyr got worse and worse. He used to get out of bed and try to run away. My father constantly kept watch at his bedside.

In that same village my elder sister was living with her mother-in-law. From that family also only my niece, Mary, was left alive, and we brought her to stay with us. She died in our house crying, "Uncle, water, water!" Baroyr continued getting steadily worse. One evening, my father never came home. Baroyr died during the night. After the burial Father came from the graveyard looking tired and broken-hearted. He fell into his bed muttering, "I don't feel well." He stayed in bed about eight days. On the other side of the room we four brothers were all in bed, ill. Only mother was still on her feet looking after us. After eight days, my father struggled into a sitting position and began calling for his dead brother. When there was no reply he called the names of his five young nephews, and then his niece who had been left a widow. Then he said "Baroyr, my son, have you also gone?" and he turned to us four brothers who were huddled in bed sick and he looked at us as if he were trying to say something to us, but he couldn't. The saliva just dribbled out of his mouth. My mother went and made him lie down again, and thus he died. We four brothers got up, and with my mother and a few of my father's friends, we took him down to the cemetery and laid him beside Baroyr.

Hunger, sickness and lice continued to increase among the refugees. There was no one left healthy who could bury the dead. At this time my mother also fell sick. Already, there was no bread left to eat. Every day we would sell a piece of cloth for a hunk of bread and divide that up between us. If ever we had any money we would buy sour milk and bring it to our mother. We shaved all her hair off to try and save her from the lice. One day when we went out in the morning, I brought bread from the market and gave it to my elder brother to share out between us. One piece also we put by our mother's pillow. We always divided the food among us this way. Then we went up to the roof, where we could catch a little sunshine to try and cleanse ourselves from the lice. After a while my brother Yervant went down to check on my mother and found her dead in her bed. I saw him coming back up weeping and he said, "Mother is dead." I rebuked him, saying, "Why do you weep like that in front of the children? Go and bring two porters and let them take and bury her." So I sent him away, and I stayed with the children. Two Armenian porters came with a ladder. They tied my mother to the ladder and carried her out. We followed them. We went to where my father was buried, in a field below the road, and we buried my mother beside him.

We could no longer meet the rent payments for our little hovel, so we left that place and hired an empty "shop" with some other young men who were already living there. By then, we were quite recovered, and could even walk without the aid of a stick. My brother Timoteos used to carry water to the house of the telegraph office director, and thus earned his living and supported what was left of his family. I learned Arabic quite well, and began selling second-hand clothes, slippers and sheets in the open streets.

My Life As a Dealer

The epidemic in Tafilah slowly died down and people began to look for some work to do. I started working as a dealer; in other words, people I knew would give me odds and ends they had to sell. People trusted me as I did an honest job. If I sold something, I would tell them how much my wages were for selling it, and hand over all the rest. Most other dealers dishonestly kept most of the money for themselves. Each day, I would bring home whatever I earned and give it to my elder brother, who divided it among us all. Our business was done not with money, but by bargaining, exchanging wheat, flour and olive oil, dry figs and sometimes bread. If you bargained with money, you would be given Turkish bank notes, but they never accepted these notes back!

One day as I was walking down the road, I came across a woollen sack. I took this home and hid it. My brother Yervant had decided to run away from Tafilah with a friend. At that time it was illegal for us to travel from one place to another, but one night, when everyone was sleeping, Yervant and his friend left. I took the woollen sack and gave it to him for warmth, as well as a few *piastres*. They were going to try and run away to Damascus.

Timoteos lived with his master, the telegraph office director, so after Yervant left, I was left alone to care for our young brother, Sarkis. Any food I had I would take to share with him and try and cheer him up and comfort him. Those of us who had survived had to put the dead behind us and fight on.

The main work available to us now was cutting wood in the small neighbouring forest, about ten miles from us. At midnight we would rise, tie a rope round our waists, take our axes in our hands and head out to this forest. There we would cut wood until noon the next day. When we had cut and collected all we could carry, we would hurry back in order to sell it before evening. At night, we headed back to the forest for more. It was no life at all. Sometimes on the road, the Arabs would meet us, steal our load, even steal our axes and ropes, and send us home empty-handed.

We Armenians were already getting used to Arab customs. We even used to eat with our fingers, like them. In fact, my work as a dealer meant that I had occasion to eat with them many a time. "*Faddal,* Selim" they would call to me (*Faddal*: help youself; Selim: my Arab name). I never waited for the second invitation! I never needed to be asked twice!

Their main food was a hand-ground wheat that they would cook up like porridge. This they would pour into a basin; then they would make a hollow in the middle, and pour olive oil into the hollow. This was special food for when guests were present. Gathered together round the basins, they would pull up their sleeves, take a bit of the wheat, roll it in their fingers until it was a little ball and dip it into the olive oil in the middle. At first I didn't like this food and could barely manage to eat it, but I forced myself to learn, determined not to be done out of the blessing!

We had a terrible time at the hand of the Arabs. It is impossible to write all the things we suffered, or any more than a few things that stick in the memory.

Refugee Life in a Cottage

There was a refugee family in Tafilah who lived in a hovel just outside the castle. The hovel consisted of two adjoining rooms with a low ceiling and door. Inside was dark and cold, just the bare stone wall and mud floor. A mother lived there with her son and daughter. One day news reached our *mukhtar* (neighbourhood chief) that the lady had died. He wasn't feeling well that day, so he told me to find a couple of porters and go and bury the body. We reached the cottage and attempted to enter, but a terrible stench from the place stopped us. The boy seemed to have gone out, so we couldn't ask him what was going on. The lady had died several days ago, and the porters refused to go in and remove the stinking remains. I went back and told the *mukhtar*, and he promised the porters some more money, so they returned, pegged their noses and went in. They nearly came straight out again but I persuaded them to get the woman out first. Inside we found the mother and daughter, both dead, and an emaciated little boy of about 10 years old. We asked what had happened to his mother and sister, and he told us they were sleeping. We brought out the putrefied bodies, and I was amazed to see the hordes of lice on them, like ants. There were so many they had gathered in huge nests. I saw four different kinds of lice, white with black heads, thin long black lice, yellow lice, and high-tailed lice. We buried the whole lot of them with the bodies! This left the young boy alone. We warned him not to go back into the cottage. We refugees put a little money together for him and bought him a shirt and an old coat. First, we took him to the stream outside town, washed him and shaved his head, and then we put the clothes on him. At night he slept in the streets, and we tried to give him any bread we could spare. Eventually, we arranged some bedding for him in the corner of a house.

Our market consisted of a bakery and five or six other little shops, just next to the *Saray* (the government building). All the Armenians were in this area, and they used to sell and buy in this market. There were some Arab shops in the area, too, but only Arabs could do business there. There was no money involved. It was all done by bartering. Wheat and olive oil seemed to be the best currency.

The Story of How We Became Muslims

One day two *hojas* (Muslim priests) came from Damascus with white turbans on their heads and an order declaring that all Armenians should change their names and accept new Muslim names. We needed to send an application to the government saying that we wanted to become Muslims. Of course, we all objected to this. If we had wanted to be Muslim, we would have converted before being deported, and thus would have been able to remain in our own country instead of losing all our possessions. But we were given no choice. Everyone began to file an application to the government. We were called to the government office for an interview. A few of us went together. We were told to sit on the ground and repeat what they said. We parroted back their words to them, although we did not believe a word they said. We were forced into this action. To refuse the Muslim religion would have meant death.

The *hojas* declared, "I believe in one god and his prophet Muhammad." We repeated their words. They wrote down our new Muslim names and sent us away. That was the extent of our conversion to Islam. However, now that we were officially Muslims, the

Muslim officers asked if they could marry our girls. Immediately we married our girls to the young men or boys of our own nationality. There was no pastor or priest among us, so we just called together a few witnesses, repeated the Lord's Prayer and a few other ceremonies, and declared them married. After these rushed marriages we had no girls left for the officers to marry.

A few months after these events, some priests (Armenian Gregorians and some Christian Arabs) and pastors were brought to our village. They had refused to convert to Islam and were being deported. They were kept in Tafilah for a few days, then taken to a distant village, where they were imprisoned and kept hungry. There in their dark prison cell with no hope for any human help they steadfastly turned their sights upward, praying fervently to God. Three days later they were quite unaccountably set free! Some of them returned to Tafilah, as it was the largest village of that area.

With these priests were also some Armenians from Damascus, including Mr Mgrditch Soukiyasian, the director of Raji Tobacco in Damascus. His wife had died a few years previously. While in Tafilah he married my cousin's widow and gave her children a father's support and care. Finally, we had some priests in the village! There was a second ceremony put on for all those who had been married in haste. This time they were officially married by an Armenian priest, according to our customs and traditions.

My Experiences as a Woodcutter in the Forest of Shohek

One day the government ordered all men between 16 and 60 to cut wood in the Shohek forest. We were arrested by the *jandarmas* and each given one pound, which we used to buy shoes. Whatever change was left from this we left with our families. Our daily wage was to be a quarter of a *mijid*. I repaired my shoes, packed my clothes and the rest of the money and took my brother Sarkis to one of my relatives to be taken care of I asked them to give him one *metelik* a day, promising to send more money later. I also asked Timoteos to keep an eye on the boy, and I left.

Officially, it was paid work, but in practice we were forced to go. The forest of Shohek was about a fourteen-hour journey away on foot. There was a village nearby called Maan, and a valley beside the forest called Wadi Musa (The Valley of Moses), where the people of Israel had no water and Moses brought water out of the rock. We were told by the Arabs that the place was visited by many European tourists. There is a spring in the valley that locals claim is the very spring that came out of the rock.

We reached the forest. I was given an axe and set to work in a section with twelve men, under the charge of a sergeant. Each sergeant was told the quota of wood to be provided by his section per day. The sergeants were also Armenian refugees and were forced to work very hard. The government ration was one *oke* of flour a day, and we were promised our wage at the end of the month. We soon spent what money we had, but when the end of the month came no more was issued. Some Arabs used to come bringing food and goods to sell, but when they understood that the government was not paying our wages, they stopped. At the end of the month, when we were all expecting to be paid, they changed our ration from one *oke* of wheat flour to one *oke* of unsifted barley flour, which was full of hard barley. Every evening we burnt chunks of wood and slept around the fire. We would make a dough with the barley flour and roll it into flat cakes, which we put in the hot ashes to bake. The result was barely edible. Our mouths would be sore and painful from gnawing at it. I suffered a lot from painful sores in my mouth. But it was impossible to run away. Guards were posted all around the forest. Any attempt to escape was considered rebellion against the government and the offender was shot by the soldiers, no questions asked, by order of the government. No one ventured near the edges of the forest.

I no longer had the strength to wield an axe. I asked the sergeant to be given the task of sawing instead. I was given a long saw, and with another workmate I would saw down the huge trees. The wood-cutters would then cut the branches off, and then we sawed the trees into three parts. The very large pieces would be blown with dynamite. The pieces were then carried by donkeys to the station about six miles away and delivered to the officers there.

One day, we were not issued with our usual ration of flour. The next day again no flour ration was given. By this time we were weak with hunger and had no strength left to work. We began to eat the tender leaves of the trees, called *melengach*. All working sections were given the same starvation treatment. Apparently the mill lacked the time and workers to grind the flour. Eventually, the rations were resumed and we hurriedly baked our dough and ate the brittle cakes.

Almost three and a half months had passed. Our clothes were in tatters from the bushes and branches in the forest. My left sleeve had completely torn off, leaving my shoulder bare. It soon burnt under the sun and the skin began to peel. All this time the lice were still our faithful companions, causing us considerable discomfort in the night. The only remedy against them was to take our clothes off and hold them over the fire until they were very warm, then vigorously shake and beat them until the lice fell into the fire. But the eggs would cling obstinately to the clothes, so that the next day the whole painful process began again. How we suffered at the hands of those lice!

Chicken Blindness in the Forest

One evening, just before going to sleep, I took a few steps into the forest and noticed that I couldn't see the trees. I went back and told my mates. Some experienced men among them told me I had chicken blindness. They advised me not to go out at night, as I would only bump into the trees. For some time I was almost blind at night, even on bright moonlit nights. The moon was a hazy red glow to me.

One day an Arab came and told us he had shot a wild pig, and we could buy it. We bargained a price for it, and he showed us from a distance where he had shot it. He himself wouldn't touch it, as it was an unclean animal and therefore a sin for Muslims to touch. Two of us went to fetch it in. I bought two *okes* of pork and also used the skin to make sandals for myself. A few days later the Arab came back saying he had shot another pig. We bought that one, too. Again, I bought two *okes* of pork, which I roasted and ate. There was no salt, unfortunately, but we made do! The pork saved me. After a few days I noticed my eye-sight had improved again and I was able to see at night.

I was convinced that if I stayed much longer in that forest I was going to die there. I had no clothing, no shoes apart from my pig-skin sandals, and my diet was still one *oke* of brittle, husk-filled barley flour. Sometimes they would give a little salt in addition. On top of this the workload was desperately heavy and my body was not used to such gruelling manual labour. I felt physically exhausted. One day I told my mate that I was going to escape to Tafilah. He was older than me and urged me not to go. The soldiers would certainly find and shoot me. I replied that I didn't care. If I stayed, it would only be a matter of days before I died anyway. If they shot me, they would put me out of my misery a few days sooner. But if I reached Tafilah I could rest there a few days. At last, my friend agreed and we decided to run away together. He told some other friends, and soon there was a small group of us planning to escape.

Escape to Tafilah

At night, in the moonlight, after everyone had gone to sleep, four of us left our places and began to walk through the forest. At last we came to the edge. I gathered the group around and told them to sit still. We were facing the valley, which was guarded on both sides. We could see the guards from where we were. I told the others that they were to wait there until I had passed and then follow, one at a time. So I went ahead a little, then sat down and waited for them to join me one by one. We escaped the guards' notice and began to walk more briskly. There was another danger point ahead of us. About two hours further down the road was a station, which we had to pass. We passed that safely from below and then began to hurry, so as to reach Tafilah before sunrise. It was a fourteen-hour journey on foot. Soon the sun rose, and we were unable to enter the village in daylight. We were forced to go into the mountains and we hid there, about ten minutes away from the village, until sunset. Had we been seen, we would have been reported to the government. We had taken only a small crust of bread with us, so we spent that day fasting. When evening came, we went into the village and everybody went to their home. Now I faced a dilemma: where should I go? I knocked on the door of Mr Mgrditch Soukiyasian. His wife, Mrs Yefkin, came and asked, "Who is it?"

"It's Smpat. Open the door," I replied. When I went in, Mr Mgrditch was amazed to see me.

"Have you come back from the grave? What happened to you?" I replied that I was merely sun-burnt. I had thrown my coat away, as it had been impossible to wear it in that heat. My shirt was torn and worn out, and my shoulders were bare. I must have looked like a savage!

Mr Mgrditch asked me if I was hungry. "Of course," I replied, upon which they brought out bread and sour-cream, which I devoured like a starved animal! They asked me to stay the night but I replied that I would lodge with an Arab I knew. If I was found in this house, they would only take me away again, but if they found me in the Arab's home, the Arab wouldn't hand me over to the authorities, and the government officials wouldn't dare to invade his home. "Even the villagers are afraid of him," I said, and bidding them a good night, I left.

My Arab acquaintance was an elderly father with three sons, all three of whom were robbers and murderers. They would head out together and sometimes return two or three days later, bringing their booty with them. They would bring German or English rifles and hundreds of cartridges. I explained my predicament to the old man. He told me not to be afraid. There was an old oven on his roof and one side of it was full of straw. I could sleep there.

The oven was the size of a huge pot. There was a narrow opening at the top, and a lid made of mud. They would burn manure around it to keep it warm, and at night they would clear away the ashes and open up the lid, and the inside would be very hot. They would place bread-dough inside and cover the lid again. In just a few minutes the bread would be baked.

So there I was, with a hot oven on one side and straw on the other side, and nothing to lie on or to cover myself with. I looked around and noticed something under the straw. When I pulled it out, it turned out to be an old donkey saddle. I spread it out on the ground, smoothed it down and slept on it. I spent half the night deliriously thinking I was back in my forest life, but at least now my stomach was full!

I spent half the night re-living my old forest life, and the other half contemplating my stomach, which was now full, and the fact that no-one would call me to work in the morning. I was happy, but still I could not sleep. My old companions, the lice, having remained hidden all day, came out again at night to trouble me. There was no forest fire to hold my clothes over now. When the lice's feet get warm, they can't grip onto the clothes and they fall into the fire. But I couldn't do that now. If I took my clothes off, I would get cold and sick. What could I do? I lay on my back and the lice began to swarm over my chest and arms. I gathered them into the hollow of my stomach, scooped them up with three fingers and flung them into the oven. I repeated this performance several times, and finally went to sleep.

My place was comfortable. In the morning, the woman came to bake the bread. She put the dough into the oven and while she was waiting for it to bake we began to chat.

I think she felt quite sorry for me, exclaiming "*Ya muhajir*! [Oh, refugee!]" I was as impatient as she for the bread to come out of the oven! Beautiful white bread! I was sure she would give me some, but kept saying over and over to myself, "If only she would give me a whole one" – which she did! I was the luckiest man alive! I had finally been saved from the barley bread!

I asked the man to go to my brother Timoteos and tell him my story and my whereabouts. Timoteos was overjoyed to see me. We talked for a while. I told him to tell no-one I was here but to find a way to bring Sarkis to me. Finally, Sarkis came too. I gave him what was left of the bread and then I gave him some money and told him to buy some food but not to mention to anyone that I had come. He brought the food and we ate together before I sent him back to his place. This pattern continued for 15 days. But my friends who had escaped with me were caught, beaten and sent back to the forest. After 15 days Izzet Pasha, the son of the *sharif*, attacked the forest, and all the soldiers and refugees ran away to Tafilah. At that time I came out of hiding.

Chapter 3

Experiences in Tafilah

The Sharif

The *sharif* was from Mecca. He was a great sheikh prince or chief there, and had much influence over the Arabs. He was also much liked among the Arab community. He had four sons, all of whom were well educated. Every *sharif* had at least 500 soldiers under his command, and some had more, according to the need of those areas. The soldiers were from different areas, but were all under British rule fighting against the Turks. Under Izzet Pasha's command they captured the forest, leaving no-one behind.

After a brief time of rest, I resumed my work as a dealer. Tafilah was ruled by an army officer with about 20 - 25 *jandarmas* under his command. The sergeant was a man called Mouri Chavoush, a wicked, domineering Albanian who extorted bribes from everyone. He used to tell us Armenians, "I am your god. No-one can save you out of my hands." Whenever he saw me, he would shout after me, "You infidel swine! Where were you?"

"In the forest," I would reply, but he would shake his head and say, "I searched for you constantly. If I had found you, I would have bound your hands, beat you and sent you back."

I used to go frequently to the market for business, and he would often summon me and make me work for him free of charge, sending me here and there to buy or bring brandy for him, or take meat to his home.

Unfortunately, my place was next to the government house, because there were a number of Armenian shops there.

I heard that the friends who had escaped with me had been arrested that very same night. Before we arrived in Tafilah, on the day we had spent in the mountains, a cable had been sent to Tafilah saying, "Four refugees have escaped. Arrest immediately and send them back." Soldiers had gone that same night to their homes with the *mukhtar*, bound them, beat them and sent them back. They had searched for me for a long time with the *mukhtar*, but could not find me.

Tafilah, as a Dealer

Now I had a shirt on my back again. I went back to the dealer's work. I had clothes, and was able to make a small living. So I left the Arab's house and took the bedding I had left in an Armenian's house and took lodgings together with my brother Sarkis.

Eight or ten days later, I noticed the *jandarmas* rounding up Armenians again. I thought about running away, but was unable to, and again I was arrested. I was given permission to arrange and settle my affairs. I gave the clothes back to their owners and Sarkis took some to another person to look after. I took a carpet (an ordinary one, not a Persian one) to sleep in, and a bag of food supplies, tied to my back.

We began to march. By evening we had reached the station. There I met a man I knew from before. He asked me where I was going and I replied that I was going to the forest.

"Who will you work with?" he asked.

"Wherever the government sends me," I told him.

I was told that the government was in great need of wood and was paying money for the wood and for the labourers. There were about 5,000 men working in the forest. Refugees had been gathered from many areas and put to work there. They had been working for some time.

The man with whom I was talking was a contractor. Every day he delivered several tons of wood. There were many contractors like him, who were paying higher wages and trying to get work from other contractors.

"Don't go anywhere," he told me, "Work for me. I'll pay you whatever you ask and I won't send you to the forest. You'll work right here, chopping the big pieces, weighing the wood and delivering orders." I accepted the proposal, and asked him to give me a sum in advance, so he opened his bag, and I noticed he was not at all low on cash!

"I'll give you 9 *mijid* now," he said. So I took the money and the following morning I set to work. I had two whole pounds, and the possibility of more if I needed it! What else could I ask for?

I worked for five or six days. The nights were cold. It was not at all like the forest, where we had burnt big pieces of wood. There was no tent to sleep in. We used to sleep huddled around the fire, but it was very windy so one side would burn and the other would freeze. I wondered how to improve my conditions, and eventually I hit upon the idea of digging a pit in the ground, just my size. At night, I put half the carpet in the pit, lay in it and covered myself with the remainder. That way I was sheltered from the wind. At first everyone laughed at me, but they were soon copying my idea!

And then my boss sent me to the forest. The large pieces of wood needed to be blown with dynamite to make them smaller. I went with two other men. We would make a hole in the tree trunk, fill it with dynamite, explode it, and carry away the pieces. There was plenty of food now: good flour and other things to eat with the bread. We were quite happy. But it lasted only a month.

At the end of the month my contractor sent me to another location.

"I've got men working on that hillside over there," he said, pointing. "Go and work with them."

Next morning, after breakfast, I rolled up my carpet and food bag, tied them to my back, and began the trek through the forest. As I was walking, I noticed two Arabs on horseback in front of a tent. Then I looked at the hillside and noticed that everybody was running away. Turkish soldiers were running in my direction. I asked them what was going on, but received no reply. "Well, everyone else is escaping. I think I'd better run away too," I said to myself, and began to run in the direction of the station. It was then that I spotted an Arab riding after me at great speed. He caught me up, took the carpet off my back and took off. I thought all that trouble was just for my carpet and, perhaps unwisely, chased after him, crying,

"Oh, chief! My food is in that carpet!" He threw the bag of food back at me, but the carpet was gone.

Then I heard that the *sharif* had attacked the forest again and all the workmen there were escaping. The *sharif's* soldiers had already reached the station. But I couldn't run away. Our station was in the valley and we did not hear about the attack until it was too late. By the time I was aware of what had happened, the road was already closed.

I came back to my mates and found them still working. I told them what was going on, that the hills around us were teeming with soldiers. They promptly stopped working, but it was impossible to escape. We decided to get all our belongings together and hand ourselves over to the Arabs. There were five or ten Arab tents on the mountainside, and the Arabs were neutral. Eight of us, taking a bag of flour, went to the chief. He received us and allowed us to stay in the guest tent. In the evening they gave us *ayran* (sour milk) in an earthen pot. We all sipped from it in turn, Arab style.

At night, the young men returned. They had been out looting with the *sharif's* men, robbing the Turkish soldiers, and had returned laden with spoils. When they saw us the young men turned on the chief's sons saying "These men are rebels! They were cutting wood for the Turkish government. Send them away from the tents. We'll go after them and kill them in the forest." The chief and his sons replied that we had come and surrendered to them, it would be a disgrace for them to kill us. The argument continued for some time and all the time we could understand everything they were saying! Imagine how we were trembling! Eventually, the chief sent everyone to their tents. We sat silently in our tent. That night we quietly agreed that if anyone escaped alive they were to go to our families conveying news of our deaths and our love. Nobody slept.

In the middle of the night I saw a bayonet at the foot of our tent. We fell upon each other and cried out to the chief for mercy. The chief came, but found no-one near our tent.

Early in the morning the chief prepared his household and took us to the castle of Shoebek, about five hours journey away, and handed us over to the Turkish soldiers there. We stayed there for one day and the next day were taken back to Tafilah, where our loved ones had given us up for dead and lost all hope of ever seeing us again.

Tafilah Again

On arriving in Tafilah I heard that my brother Timoteos had received a telegram from our brother Yervant, with news that he was in Nablus working as a tailor. He had also sent some money. We were overjoyed to hear that he was alive. We had had no news from him since he had left. Then Timoteos left the house where he was staying and went to Karak (in Biblical Moab), a day's journey from Tafilah.

One day while I was walking near the palace I saw Nouri Chavoush talking with the Armenian *mukhtar*. They called me over and asked me to take about 300 lambs to the railway station. That was where we had been detained and held without being given any water. At first I refused to go. "You'll send me to the station and the next day, when I'm too exhausted to resist, you'll send me to the forest," I argued. There was a rumour that they were recruiting for the forest again.

Nouri Chavoush swore at me by way of reply. He said, "You'll go all right, you swine. You'll go like an ass!" After that, what could I do? I tried begging. Finally, after a lot of talking, he promised not to send me to the forest.

"May the Lord grant you long life," I said, and left.

I took some bread and salt with me. There was another Armenian coming with me who knew a little bit about shepherding and he took a knife, too. We reached the door of the fold at about midnight. Two *jandarmas* were also with us.

After midnight we began to walk, one of us leading the flock and one of us in the rear. The *jandarmas* also accompanied us on horseback.

We were told to take good care of the animals, because they would get tired and might get left behind. In the morning all the lambs were still with us. At noon we sat near a spring, ate our bread and rested. After a while we began to walk again, but still no lamb got left behind. Then my mate hit one of the lambs on the leg and it fell to the ground. We informed the *jandarmas*, who told us to cut off the head and give it to them so they could present it to the officer at the station; the flesh we put in our own bags. After a while the lambs could no longer walk because of the heat and a number of them fell in the road. The heads were given to the *jandarmas* and the flesh to us. We shared some of the meat with the *jandarmas*. At night we roasted the meat well at the station and shared it with some Arabs from Tafilah who were also there. That night we remained there in a hut. Early the next morning we began to travel with the Arabs, who also gave us donkeys to ride on, and in the evening we arrived safely in Tafilah.

Back to the Forest

One day I saw the *jandarmas* were arresting Armenians again. They arrested me as well and took me to the *Saray*. It was a strict order. The train wasn't working but wood had been demanded urgently. Many were arrested, even blind and lame men.

Nouri Chavoush came in and put us into three lines. He marched up and down these lines and each time he beat someone, usually the old, blind or lame, and then let them go. I kept looking into his eyes, but I was left standing in my place. Then he came to me, caught my ear and pulled it.

That was fine by me, so long as he let me go. While I was running, the officer thought I was running away. He sent a *jandarma* after me, who demanded, "Where do you think you are going?" I replied that Nouri Efendi had sent me away, whereupon they called Nouri Efendi, and he confirmed that I was to be set free. I couldn't express what joy I felt! The following morning the rest of the men were sent to the forest. They returned some time later, exhausted, and many were wounded. Then the troops of Izzet Pasha re-captured the forest and no-one was sent there any more.

Turkish Soldiers at Tafilah

One day I saw a regiment of Turkish soldiers, known as the Cavalry of the Legion of Spears. There were over 300 mounted soldiers. They had escaped from the fighting at Wadi Serar, and were intending to go to Damascus, but had got lost en route! They stayed at Tafilah a few days.

It happened that at that time an Arab had stolen a handkerchief from me. So I went and reported him to these soldiers. The soldiers had no great love for the Arabs at that time. In many cases Arabs had fought against the Turks. So they arrested this Arab and imprisoned him in one of the rooms in the *Saray* as revenge. He was badly beaten. He immediately sent for his wife to find the handkerchief and return it to me. Instead, the wife threw a stone at me from behind. Had it hit me, it would have killed me instantly. I remember feeling glad that I had caused the Arab to be beaten. But the other Arabs all warned me, "If that man sees you again he will kill you." I was never again able to walk down that particular street!

The Argument Between the Mukhtar of Tafilah and the Sharif

We heard one day that our village chief, the *mukhtar*, had gone to the *sharif*. He was actually the *mukhtar* of a number of villages, and had a number of other *mukhtars* under him. He was a wealthy man, much honoured among the Arabs. He was often able to use his influence to settle difficulties and problems without taking them to the government. People were always applying to him when they were in difficulties.

He had received 2000 pounds in return for an agreement that the men under his authority would not join the Turkish troops to fight against the *sharif*'s army.

A few days later we heard that Izzet Pasha had come with troops and captured the *mukhtar*'s farm, about three hours' journey away. The following morning the government sent messages to the Arabs, saying that all Arabs would unite with *jandarmas* to fight against the *sharif*. The *jandarmas* went out and after a while the Arabs joined them. I was near the *Saray* at that time. A sergeant came from the scene of battle.

"Sir," he said, "All these Arabs are just shooting into the air."

Nouri Chavoush ordered the *jandarmas* to stand to one side. We were warned to make trenches under the windows of the *Saray* and around the building, as defence. Then the *sharif's* army came with the native Arabs.

We ran away to the *Saray* and watched the scene from a nearby house. The Arabs came and hoisted the Arab flag up over the *Saray*. They began to take the *jandarmas'* horses. Nouri Chavoush shot one of the Arabs. In response the Arabs started breaking the windows and doors of the *Saray* in order to rob the building. I saw them capture the *jandarmas* as well as Nouri Chavoush. His hat had fallen off and his coat was torn. The natives wanted to kill him, but the *sharif's* soldiers did not deliver him up to them. They took him to the *sharif's* camp out on the mountain.

One day they gave Nouri Chavoush a skin bottle and told him to bring water from the village. He begged not to be sent back to the village, but to no avail. They told him to bring wood and twigs to burn, and sent him off with a guard. A young Armenian man saw him gathering wood, and he helped him to make a bundle with it and load it on his back. The Armenian was also gathering wood to load and take away. As he followed Nouri Chavoush he chanted behind him, "Cho, pig cho, get out of my sight." (Arabs used this expression to the donkeys who carried their loads for them.) Nouri Chavoush was furious at this, but he was powerless to act. The tables had been turned.

A few days later the officers were sent to Akaha and from there to Egypt, to the prison camp.

Chapter 4

Under Occupation

Tafilah under the Rule of the Sharif

After this event the Armenians felt much more free and happy. The *sharif's* purse was full of English gold pounds and there was plenty of work. The *sharif's* men had been in Allaha for a long time, and had had no opportunity to spend their money. Here in Tafilah they began to open their purse strings and spend. Armenian men and women were kept busy making clothes, shirts handkerchiefs and other articles for them. Everyone was employed. I was also busy with dealing work, but this time with a slight difference; now I was actually receiving money for the business I did!

One day as I was working a group of the *sharif's* officers approached me and commissioned me to find brandy for them.

"You'll probably find some belonging to the refugees," they said. "Bring us some and we'll pay whatever you ask for it." I was afraid to take on this new commission, because selling brandy was forbidden by the government, but they were persistent. "We'll give you a whole pound if you find half an *oke* for us," they said, and on hearing the word "pound" my fear suddenly dissipated!

"Very well, I'll bring it," I replied.

The soldiers I had bargained with were Turks, who had escaped from the prison camp and returned to the *sharif's* army, where they lied about their nationality. They had joined as sergeants but had been promoted to officers and were living well with good pay.

I went to the Armenians and asked around to see if anyone had some brandy. Naturally I found some and took it back to the soldiers, who paid me accordingly. I asked around for more, but there was obviously none left, so two enterprising Armenians immediately took a few skin bottles and dry figs, formed a partnership and began producing brandy. They made brandy-pans by opening a small hole in the lid of each pan and connecting a tin pipe to it. Each pan made one *oke* of brandy. It was forbidden for us to approach the soldiers' camp, but being a dealer I had certain dispensations, such as being allowed as far as the outer post. But here, the soldiers didn't know who the brandy was intended for, and delivering to the wrong person could lead to arrest. So I was allowed in camp to sell my produce.

This time, we divided the profits between us and soon we had a thriving business going. But it didn't last long. Our brandy production site was reported to the government, who destroyed the place. As it was a first offence the producers were not fined, merely warned not to be caught doing it again. We never re-started the trade because Arabs don't like brandy. They have a wholesome fear of drunkards. They never had breweries. Anyone desiring brandy had to make it in their own homes for their own use, not for sale.

I continued my work as a dealer. This time I was buying and selling English and German rifles. This business was very profitable and had a quick turnover. I was making good money.

We never had sugar or rice as refugees. But when the *sharif* came, his soldiers all had sugar and rice, and soon some found its way to refugee homes too.

I was walking with the *mukhtar* one day, with two rifles on my shoulder and a hundred cartridges for each one, for sale. Overhead,

I saw two German planes in the sky. The *mukhtar* took one of the rifles from my shoulder and a few cartridges and shot at it. It was not forbidden in those days to shoot a rifle. I took the other one and shot a few rounds. We were in an open space, but were using the *mukhtar's* wall as a defence. Then we saw that the plane had opened fire on us with its machine gun. At first we only felt something like tiny stones coming at us, and we thought the *mukhtar's* son was throwing pebbles at us. Then we suddenly realised it was coming from the plane. It was too high to have any effect. We went to another place near the ammunition store, but the *mukhtar* didn't allow us to linger there, in case a bomb was dropped on the ammunition. Instead we went into the trees outside the village. All the time I was looking up at the plane, and never noticed when my companion went away from me. Suddenly something white began to shine from the plane. "He's dropped a bomb!" I cried, and ran away.

There was a road beside the trees, only a few steps away. I jumped quickly down there seconds before the bomb fell with a deafening roar. I felt all the pieces of the bomb fly over my head. I was terrified. The *mukhtar* thought I was crushed to pieces. He came to the tree where I had been standing a second before and saw that a great branch of the tree was broken and I was nowhere in sight. He began searching everywhere for bits of my body. All the time I was lying silently on the ground, shaken. Finding no bits of body or any other signs of death the *mukhtar* decided I must still be alive and began calling my name, "Smpat! Smpat!" I could hear the voice, but I couldn't answer. Finally, I leaned on the wall and threw a branch to catch his attention. He saw me, ran over, and pulled me up. He kept asking me questions and still I couldn't answer. I was pale as death and much shaken. So he took me to the spring, washed my face and then took me home and gave me lemonade. With rest and time the shock passed and I found my tongue again.

The Battle of the Sharif's Soldiers

One day we heard that Turkish soldiers were marching from Karak to capture Tafilah. There were about 800 of them, fully equipped and with all their provisions. The *sharif's* guard had seen them and sent a message to Tafilah. All the soldiers of Tafilah were prepared for battle. Then, according to Arab custom, a public crier went around the town crying for all to come and help. I saw that all the Arab civilians took up arms and went to fight against the Turks. The two sides met in a valley and fought until sunset. The Turks were defeated. About 200 were taken prisoner and some ran away, back to Karak. The Arabs took the prisoners' uniforms and put them on themselves, then gave their own shirts to the prisoners. The prisoners came to Tafilah in nothing but these white shirts. It was very cold and many were shivering. One cold, rainy day they were sent on to Akaha and from there to the prison camp in Egypt. Many died en route.

Two or three days after this battle the Turks attacked again, this time with German soldiers. Again, all the *sharif's* men went out to fight. This time they were defeated. The survivors escaped to the mountains. A messenger was sent to those who had remained at Tafilah instructing them to blow up the ammunition store and run away. The Armenians managed to get hold of some rifles before the stores were burnt. The *sharif's* soldiers also opened the food stores and told the Armenians to take away as much food as they could. Native Arabs also took as much as they could carry and ran away to the mountains. Only the Armenians were left in the village, and those Arabs who had been too afraid to come out of their houses and flee.

All the Armenians began to take food from the stores to their homes: bags of rice, sugar, dates, skin bottles full of oil. Some of the Armenian men escaped with the Arabs. I also went with them for about half an hour, but was obliged to turn back because of my brother Sarkis. These young Armenians eventually went to Egypt.

The Armenians were left alone in the village. There was plenty of food. Days passed and still the Turks did not come to occupy the village. Gradually, Arabs began to return. Then we learnt that Arabs had attacked Armenian homes further down the street and taken all the food. The Armenians had tried to defend themselves, so the Arabs had climbed on to the roof and opened fire down the chimney. A woman and child had been killed and one man wounded. Finally, they had opened the door and the Arabs had taken everything.

At our house everyone was drinking brandy to cheer themselves up. I was at another house, doing some business there. As I was returning home, climbing a steep hill near a big dunghill in the middle of the road, I saw the Arab whom I had reported to the Turkish soldiers and who had had a good beating because of me. He pointed the rifle at me and moved to pull the trigger.

"Don't shoot me!" I called quickly. "I have money; I can give you money. What will you gain by killing me?"

I was overheard by the *mukhtar*'s mother. "That man is going to kill Smpat," she cried. The *mukhtar* came out drunk, with a rifle in his hand.

I turned to the Arab. "Now what are we going to do?" I said. "This man is drunk. He'll kill us both." Arabs are afraid of drunkards. The sight of the drunk *mukhtar* with a rifle in his hand was too much for him. He left me and ran. His purpose had not been to kill me, but to rob me. But I had been saved from this, too. I got home at evening time. That same evening ten or twelve Arabs came with their donkeys and took all our sugar, rice and other foodstuffs we had brought from the store. To resist would be fatal. The following day Turkish soldiers came and occupied the village.

Under Turkish Occupation Again

Again, persecution started for the Armenians. All the men were set to work carrying telegraph poles on their shoulders to erect on the Karak road. A few days later the order came for Armenians to prepare to be taken to Karak. The following morning was rainy. We began our walk to Karak. Everyone was forced to go, including the women and children, the blind, lame and elderly. We were allowed to take only a little water and some bread with us. A few had managed to bring a blanket as well. It rained for over two hours, and the road was very muddy. Then the sun shone again and our clothes dried. We walked until evening, although the journey usually would take us only four to five hours. At night we went into a big cave, made a fire, burnt the telegraph poles we had previously carried, and passed the night there.

The next day we started again early. At the same time, Turkish soldiers also started out. There were cavalry and privates with truckloads of ammunition and provisions. They passed us en route, but when they arrived at the plains the mist and fog were so thick that they lost their way and got bogged down in the mud.

The night was foggy and wet. But when we awoke the next morning the sun was shining beautifully. As we began to walk, we passed many soldiers who had frozen, and sunk in the mud. Cannon and mules were also stuck in the mud. We were amazed at the wonderful way God had helped us refugees, travelling with our women and children in safety over a road where tough young soldiers with all their equipment and provisions had frozen.

After a very difficult journey, particularly because of the mud, we finally arrived in the village. I was carrying Sarkis on my shoulders. I saw one of our relatives, a widow lady, looking for her son. She asked me if I had seen him, but I couldn't help her. She thought that he was walking at the front, but it turned out that he must have been walking at the end of the caravan. She begged me to turn back and look for him. So I left Sarkis with her and went back. I walked for about fifteen minutes and found the widow's son, stuck in the mud. I tried to pull him out, but I couldn't. Even his hands were stuck, and he was crying. Finally I got him out, lifted him onto my shoulders and brought him to his mother. He was about eight years old.

That night we slept in a stable in the village. The next day we arrived at Karak. There was a big, half-built school building there. There were no shutters on the doors and windows. At first we stayed in this building, but afterwards we managed to rent houses and live in the town. There were other Armenian refugees there, who had settled in Karak two years earlier.

A Few Words about Karak

Karak is a large village on top of a hill, surrounded on all sides by deep valleys. The village itself is a castle. Its inhabitants used to wear a white shirt that came down to their feet. Over it they wore a long, wide garment called a *mashleh*, and their head was covered with a long white headscarf, over which they wore an *agil*. Long, woven locks of hair hung down on both sides of this. The women also were barefooted and wore only a long, dark blue dress that came down to their feet. They would spread their bed upon the earthen ground and cover themselves with the *mashleh*, or a carpet. Only the very rich had a bed made of wood, on which they spread a kind of hay called *yavshan*, which has a lovely smell. A carpet would be laid on this hay, and the bed was fit for a king!

Most of the population were Muslims, though there were some Orthodox Arabs, too. There were two Orthodox churches, and a large mosque. I found my brother Timoteos living in Karak. He was working on the farm of a rich, Orthodox Arab family. His boss was a very respected man, a man of conscience and of a good character. Timoteos would transport necessities for them with a donkey, and worked willingly for them. The Turkish government soon evacuated Karak as well. The rule was given to an Arab Muslim *mukhtar* called Erfefan.

Karak under Arab Rule

The new *mukhtar* quickly gave governmental positions to his own men. Others were made policemen, commanders and officers. Of course, he was not fit to rule. He thought only of one thing: how to make money. Every day he ordered the arrest of men, women and children in the refugee camps, and imprisoned them in the castle. This castle was a big ruin, full of snakes, thorns, and dirt. There was nowhere even to sit, let alone stay. Anyone complaining was simply given a good thrashing. There was no-one to plead our case. On payment of one *mijid*, you could be set free. Anyone who couldn't pay would stay there, hungry. This performance was repeated every day.

One day a few Arabs attacked the house where I was staying. My brother Sarkis and I were arrested and taken to the castle. There were many other Armenians there. After staying a while I paid two *mijid* and was set free. Another day an Arab confronted me in the street. He took a dagger out of his belt and pointed it at my chest. I didn't recognise him at first, but suddenly I realised it was the same Arab whom I had reported to the Turkish soldiers in Tafilah, and caused to have a beating. I began to beg for my life, offering him a *mijid*. At just that moment Timoteos's boss came by. When he saw that I was being attacked by this stranger from Tafilah, he took out his own dagger and attacked him, crying, "So, you've come all the way from Tafilah to kill our men here!" At this the Arab took to his heels.

Fighting soon broke out between the Muslims of Karak and the Orthodox Christian Arabs. Both sides were shooting each other. The Christian Arabs gathered in the church and fortified the place.

There was a fear that Muslims would attack the Christians' living quarters, where, of course, the Armenian refugees were also living. That night we heard bullets flying around us. The question that hung in the air for us all was, "Where can we go?" One of our Muslim neighbours had a large chicken shed, and we decided to go there. No one saw us creeping out at dead of night. About eight of us squashed into this little shed, and there we sat on top of each other and waited until the morning, when we crept back to our own homes. The next day other Arabs came from surrounding villages and re-established the peace.

Still under Arab Rule

The soldiers of Erfefan arrested me again and took me to the castle. Sarkis was with me. We stayed for a while, until I paid two *mijid* and was released. This was repeated every two to three days. *Mukhtar* Erfefan, our ruler, was eager to get his hands on our money as quickly as possible but he did nothing for our benefit.

One day I went to my brother Timoteos. "Please," I said, "ask your master to give Sarkis a position too. I can't keep going like this. If I am free from taking care of Sarkis, I can avoid them and they will not catch me again." The master accepted and I sent Sarkis to Timoteos. The master was a very good man. I used to talk things over with him sometimes. He got to love my brothers very much, and at last my mind was at rest concerning Sarkis.

One day Arabs spotted me in the street and began calling after me, "Stop, *muhajir* (refugee)!" As soon as I saw them I ran away and climbed up on a roof. I kept on running over the roofs (Arab roofs are flat and joined to one another, so you can walk from one roof to another) until I reached the house of an Orthodox Arab. The man knew me well and I stayed with him a few hours, until my pursuers were gone. Many others were arrested that day, so they were not too concerned about the fate of one *muhajir*. Every day the persecution and cruelty toward the refugees increased, until we could no longer bear it. Soon they began beating and flogging those who could not pay, as if trying to beat the required money out of us. By now, the price was no longer one *mijid*, but whatever was found on our persons.

Chapter 5

Escape to Hebron

Escape

One day we heard that the *sharif's* army, led by one of his sons, were occupying the plains of the Dead Sea, about 40 to 50 miles from Karak. A party of Armenian refugees had already reached there in safety, a few hundred in number, with their families and two hired Arab guides. They had left Karak at night and the guards brought a letter back from them, saying that they were all well and urging us to escape and join them. On receiving this letter we also hired two guides, one Muslim and one Christian Arab. We bargained for the price of 200 *mijid* to be taken safely to the *sharif*. About 200 of us prepared to escape that night. I sent a message to Timoteos and Sarkis to come that day, without telling their master. We all gathered in one house, along with the guides, who were fully armed. We collected the money to give them. I slept a while, until everyone was ready, as the plan was to walk all night. I was dressed like an Arab, covered with a *mashleh*, and with an *agil* on my head. I woke in the night to the cries of two Arabs leaning over me shouting, "Cursed refugees!" They began to beat me. I saw that they were Erfefan's soldiers. I got up, put on my *mashleh*, and began to shout

with them, "Cursed refugees!" (Arabs liked that expression.) There
was a dilapidated wall next to the door. I climbed onto that and sat
down. About eleven Arabs had come to arrest us, among them our
two guides. I could hear the whistle of the whips and cries for mercy.
What could I do? They did not touch my brothers, because they
were very young, and they did not touch the women. They made
everyone promise not to run away to the *sharif*, took some money,
and left. I went back in. Everyone was sitting quietly. One of them
turned to me and commented, "You had a lucky escape!" I replied,
"God is merciful. This hour too will pass."

A merchant from Marash was there, Mr Hagop Dolabjian, an
acquaintance of mine and a friend of my father. I went to see him
and asked how he was. He smiled at me, though his heart was weeping. "I got a good thrashing!" he replied. We all visited him the next
day. Two days later he died. After that his wife and children became
very poor.

They faced some pretty miserable times later on. Their great
desire was to escape to Jerusalem, where the chief priest had promised to look after them. But they had spent all their money. They
had only one American cheque left, and nobody could buy this.
There was no bank in Karak, and the Arabs did not recognise the
cheque. Finally, an Arab bought it at a very low price. I asked the
woman why she had sold it at such a low price, and she replied that
it was better to sell cheap than to beg. "If only we could escape to
Jerusalem," she said, "My brother-in-law would look after us, and
my son would send money from America."

Eight days passed. Again we were preparing to escape.
Everything was prepared during the day. Timoteos and Sarkis were
far away from us on a farm, about three hours away. I went to their
master in Karak and told him to send the boys to me. "You go by
yourself and be free," he replied. "The boys are all right on the farm.
Don't disturb their comfort. When peaceful times come, I myself
will bring them to Jerusalem. They are not the only Armenians on

my farm." I knew that what he was saying was true, and I had his assurance that he would bring the boys to Jerusalem and take them to the Armenian monastery there. In any case, Timoteos did not want to leave his master and run away. "He loves me like a son," he said to me. But I was still not satisfied with this assurance. I gave a pound to a young man to go to the farm and tell the boys to come. He knew where they were, but refused to go.

I didn't want to miss this chance to escape. There was a great party preparing to run away that night, and the only ones remaining were old and weak people. It would be difficult to run away with them, even if we did get a second chance, because our path took us trekking over mountains for several days. If I missed this chance, I was unlikely to get another. My life was in danger. So I sent a message to Timoteos by some Armenians who were left behind, and sent greetings to him and the assurance that I would do my best to get them free. The Armenians all assured me, "Don't worry about us. There are still many refugees, and your brothers will share the same fate as comes our way."

"A safe passage to Jerusalem is my only wish for us all," I replied.

Journey to the Shores of the Dead Sea

We set off before the soldiers of Erfefan heard anything. Soon we had left Karak behind and were walking down into a valley, then up the opposite mountain. There we were spotted by a group of Arabs, about nine in all, who cried after us, "Hey! *Muhajir*, where are you going?"

Unable to deny the truth, we admitted, "We are going to the *sharif*."

"Oh no, you're not!" they replied. "You must be rebels, escaping from Erfefan. Turn back now." The guards, afraid of what might happen, said nothing. A few shots were fired at us, to show that they meant what they said. But we knew that if we turned back to Karak they would beat us to death. We begged for mercy. So they demanded money. We all sat down in the middle of the field and began to search for money. We told the soldiers not to go near the women and children, and we collected about ten *mijid* for each of them, 90 *mijid* altogether. On receiving the money, the Arabs said, "Don't be afraid. We will take you to the *sharif.* Get up!" So we got up and after walking a while, our escort ordered us to sit down again. "No further until you give each of us five *mijid* more."

Well, what could we do? There was no escape for us. We gave them forty-five *mijid* more. Then we began to walk again. A little while later, we were ordered to sit down again. We all obeyed like sheep in a flock. Again, they each took five *mijid* more. There was hardly any money left on us at all. Fortunately, when the *sharif* had come to Tafilah, Armenian refugees had done good business and made some money, so at least we had it to buy our way to safety now.

We began to walk again until the next morning, but we were only about three hours away from Karak. The sun rose and our escort led us to a cornfield. There was an old ruin there. They said we could not walk in the daylight. We must wait in the ruin until sunset, because if the villagers saw us they would attack us and rob us. So we stayed in the ruin, with our guards. The nine Arabs were wandering around the fields. Now and again they would come to us, take some of our men and search them, taking whatever they could find: watches, pen-knives, money, clothes, and so forth. They robbed me too, but at least our women and children were left in peace. They took a lot of clothes from us, then asked us for bags, in which they put their spoils. In the afternoon they disappeared. We were left alone with our guards.

Later, we saw a man on horseback coming through the cornfield towards us. It was the village *mukhtar*. "Who are you and where are you going?" he cried.

"We are going to the *sharif,*" we replied.

"No! You must turn back."

We fell at his feet and began to cry out. Then he laughed and said, "Just joking. Go in peace," and left us. None of us found the joke very funny. But at least he went away!

In the morning we saw another Arab coming. He was barefoot, and had long hair and a long beard. Arabs don't cut their hair or beard; they just shave around their beard. He had three lines of cartridges on him and a German rifle on his shoulder. "*Muhajir*, where are you going?" he shouted.

"To the *sharif*," we replied.

"You cannot go. You are rebels. Turn back!"

What could we do? We started crying out to him, too, and so he started to demand money. "Give me five *mijid*," he said. "I will take you to the *sharif*."

"We haven't got any money," we replied. "They've even stolen most of our clothes from us."

"All right, give me ten *mijid*," he replied." Somehow, we gathered about ten *mijid* together and gave it to him. By now evening had come. "Don't be afraid," he said. "Follow me. No one will dare say anything to you."

What could we do but follow? Our guards were afraid of him. The man took us off the main road and by short cuts through the forest. All night he walked over hills and plains and we followed him. Then he ordered us to sit down. We were expecting him to ask for more money. Instead he asked for a rope and a pail. We gave these to him, and he used them to draw water from a well there, and give us all a drink. I helped him to draw up the water.

We carried on walking. "There is a village further down," our escort informed us, "and we must pass that village before sunrise. There are two parties in that village; one is on the *sharif's* side and the other is pro-Turkish. It will be better to pass that place in the dark." Unfortunately, we didn't make it; the sun rose before we approached the village, which was called Khinzera. He split us into several groups and we went round the village. Our group went up a hill and round a turn in the road, where we were ordered to sit and wait. There were about 10 to 15 of us, including women and children. We sat and waited for the rest of the group, but they didn't come. I climbed onto a big rock nearby and saw that the refugees were going into the village. Nobody was coming in our direction. Then I saw our Armenian *mukhtar* waving his handkerchief to us, bidding us to come. So we went back, and discovered that the village *mukhtar* had received them. They were all resting in a nice garden near a spring, where we joined them. A few hours later some of us went to the village and bought flour and food. The *mukhtar* advised us not to wait long there, as there might be some trouble from the villagers. "A little further down there is a grove of olive trees," he said to us. "You can stay there. You will be out of danger there," So we left the village and went to the grove of olive trees, where we were indeed out of danger that night. We made bread and other food, and rested. Our latest escort left us at Khinzera, so after that we were left with our original guides.

Early the next morning we began to walk again. Some Arabs told us that the *sharif* was near and that there was plenty of water at his camp. "When you've walked a little further," they said, "you will see the *sharif's* tents." So we didn't take any water with us. And sure enough, a little later we saw the Dead Sea, and a few houses on the plain beside it.

Our guides disappeared one by one. There is an old proverb that says, "There is no need for a guide to a village that can be seen." Our guides obviously knew this proverb and agreed with it! We went fearlessly toward the tents. But they were still quite a distance away. Noon approached, and the weather was very hot. "Water, just a little water!" was the cry from all around me, but there was no water to be had. We asked an Arab if there was any water on the way. "No," he replied, "No water." We hurried on to reach the water. Many couldn't walk because of the thirst.

Many drank their own urine, but of course, that only made them thirstier. It was every man for himself now. Those who stopped on the way just got left behind. No one was able to look after them. Those who were able to walk were trying to reach the water. One old man next to me said, "I can't go another step. You go on. I'll stay here and die." He remained there. Then a child remained, and then another. Altogether about twelve people were left behind on the way.

I had a friend called Khoren Moumjian. He was my school classmate. His mother lost her strength and could no longer walk, although she was still quite a young woman, about 45 years old. She was going to be left behind too. At that moment we saw an Arab coming. We ran to him and asked him for some water. He only had about a cupful of water in his skin-bottle, and he refused to give it to us. We tried very hard, but could not persuade him to part with it. In the end we began to threaten him and tried to use his rifle. "But if I give you the water, what shall I do then?" he asked. But we had to get that water off him. We offered him a gold ring, but again, he refused. He wanted gold money, but my friend had no money. At last we tried to persuade him that the gold ring was worth at least one gold pound. So he took the ring, and we got a small coffee cup's worth of water for it, which we poured into the woman's mouth, and then we hurried on to reach the caravan.

There was still some distance to go. This final walk in the wilderness was proving too much for us. We really needed a man of faith like Moses to bring water out of the rock for us, but unfortunately there was no-one with such gifts among our party. We were soon crying out for water again. My tongue was beginning to stick to my mouth. We walked on and on, and there was still another two hours ahead of us before we would reach the *sharif's* camp. There was a deep valley to cross. Five or six of us who were still able to walk took water bottles and began to hurry ahead, to bring water back to the others. When I reached it, I saw that it was a very small spring. I dipped my head into the water and began to drink and cool myself. Some people who had run ahead earlier were also there, in the camp. They also filled bottles of water and we rushed back to the rest of the group, who were coming slowly, parched and exhausted. We gave them all water to drink one by one.

One woman had lost her eight-year-old son. She was weeping loudly and searching everywhere for him. When we had arrived to join the others, she had thought he was among us, and carried on without him, but a little further on in the forest she discovered he was lost. We ran around searching for him, but he was nowhere to be found. His mother was still weeping. For about eight days after our arrival we searched for that boy, but found neither him nor his corpse. He was lost.

In the Sharif's Territory

The river Jordan flows into the Dead Sea. We were on the south shore of this sea, in a place called Ghor Safe (in Biblical Edom). We had nothing to fear now, neither Turkish cruelty, nor Sheikh Erfefan. We were quite comfortable, but our food had run out. We asked the *sharif* for flour, but they themselves were short of flour. Sometimes the *sharif's* soldiers brought bread and flour and secretly sold them to us.

There were about five to ten tents belonging to native Arabs on the shores of the sea by our camp. These Arabs were naked apart from a small rag that covered their shame. Each one had two or three goats, and a small patch of ground by every tent, where they grew vegetables, barley or corn. This was their livelihood, and they knew no other lifestyle. They made their tents from goat's hair, and drank goat's milk. By careful economy, they lived all year round on their corn crop. They also had a kind of delicious wild fruit called *dom*, red, as large as a cherry, with a rather sour taste. They would dry this fruit and then grind it with the hand mill.

Arab boys used to bring this dried and ground fruit to us, and we would exchange it for white buttons. For some reason these white buttons were of use to them. We even exchanged buttons, set on pieces of string, for flour.

I have mentioned previously the lady whose child had got stuck in the mud on the way to Karak and had been rescued. She was related to us. She had run out of money, and came to me, but I also had no money left. She showed me a golden bracelet she had which was worth ten gold pounds. Could I sell it for her? I began to consider whom I could sell it to. We could think of no possible customer, but hunger had left her with no other alternative but to try. She did, however, ask me not to accept less than eight pounds.

I took the bracelet straight to *Sharif* Abdallah. I asked the guard at the door of his tent for permission to enter, and was told to wait, because there was someone inside with the *sharif*. The visitor eventually came out and I was allowed to enter.

Sharif Abdallah knew Turkish very well. I bowed to him and saluted him, and he asked me, "What is it you want, friend?"

I took out the bracelet and placed it on the table. "This bracelet belongs to a widow lady," I said. "She has no money, and this is all she has left. She wants to sell this, but no one will buy it here, except for you. Unless you buy it, she and her children will go hungry today. It is worth twelve gold pounds, and is made of pure gold. I am not selling it to you. I will only give it to you as a gift, and also ask you to have mercy on this widow and her children."

The *sharif* began to think. "What am I to do with this?" he asked, picking up the bracelet.

"It is gold. You can do anything you like with it," I replied. He looked at me again, as if doubting the genuineness of the gold. I said, "Sir, in our country women wear this on their arms as an ornament." He said no more, but wrote a note and sent me to the treasurer to get money. "May the Lord give you long life, sir," I said, and went out.

I found the treasurer and handed him the note, unaware of the
quantity involved. The treasurer read the note, then took out his
money bag. All the time I was wondering how much he was going
to give. As he counted the money, my eyes followed him and I also
counted in my mind. Seven … eight … nine… He handed the
money to me, and I stayed where I was. "What's the matter?" asked
the treasurer, looking up at me.

"I'm a dealer," I replied, "and there is no change in this bag, only
gold coins. The widow lady I represent has no money at all, so how
is she going to give me my wages? Could you please take back one
of the gold coins and give me change instead?"

"I have no change," replied the treasurer. "I will give you two
rouplees for your need."

I thanked him, took the money, and left. I took one gold pound
and the two *rouplees*, but I had no pockets, or anywhere to hide the
money. So I put the money inside my shirt, like the Arabs do, and
tied it from the outside with a piece of cotton thread. The rest of it,
eight gold pounds, I gave to the widow, who was overjoyed.

Journey from the Dead Sea to Jerusalem

After about a week on the shores of the Dead Sea, the *sharif* gave
us a guide and we began to walk again.

Unfortunately, our old companions, the lice, were back to trouble us. They were not so many in number as before, but they were
enough to give us considerable irritation. We left the Dead Sea and
came to a wide plain covered in bushes. We travelled around the
shore of the sea. After that, we came to plains covered in reeds, and
then to a salt plain, where the ground was white, like snow. The sun
sank low into the earth and still we were travelling around the sea.
We spent the night in the salt plain. There was no water there, but
the guide pointed out a valley, where there was a small spring running through. But there were also wild animals in the valley. So

some of us went in crying out and shouting and making a loud noise to frighten the animals, while others drank the water, which was salty and smelt of brimstone. We took a little with us, in case of great need.

The next day we got up early in the morning, and after several hours walking we reached a small hill that the Arabs had told us about. The rocks of the hill were salty. This, we were told, was the place where Lot's wife had been turned into a pillar of salt. We went on again for many hours, and reached a place with many ruins and some trees growing round it. These, we were told, were the ruins of Sodom and Gomorrah. We sat under the trees, and prepared some food. There was a small spring there, too. As I was wandering around, I noticed a dry brook, with a wall built to channel the rain water coming down from the mountain. I followed the line of the brook, and found something that looked like a well, its mouth closed with stones. I rolled the stones back and looked in, but could not see anything. It was like a cave. Shepherds had obviously made it to store water in. I dropped a stone in, and found that it was full of water, and the water was quite high up and easy to reach. Immediately I went and told the rest of the group, and we went and drew water from this little reservoir. It was beautiful water, icy cold and refreshing. We drank our fill and filled our water-skins.

We set off again after lunch and by evening we reached Khalil Rahman (Hebron). There we saw Abraham's tomb, with a big mosque built over it. No one was allowed to go in and see it. Khalil Rahman was a nice little town. Our guide handed us over to the British authorities. It was the first time we had seen English soldiers, and we all praised God for delivering us from Turkish bondage.

Chapter 6

Journeys as a Soldier

Under British Rule

The English soldiers gave us a building to sleep in. In the yard of the building they cooked soup in big cauldrons and gave it to us with bread. The next day, we were told we were not to go out, because our clothes and bedding were going to be boiled. Some friends and I managed to escape, however, and went to the market. I took the gold that I had taken for the bracelet and changed it for money, with which I bought a set of soldier's clothes and put it on. Our clothes were not boiled. Two days later we were told that those who could walk were to begin walking to Jerusalem. The women, children and elderly were to be taken in lorries. It was eight hours' journey by foot. We began in the afternoon. There was no need for a guide, because we had nothing to fear. We were to follow the main road. Along the road we kept meeting English soldiers.

At midnight we reached the top of a hill, from where we could see the lights of a town in the distance. We continued walking with great joy. Some of the people in our group had been in this area before. They said it was the lights of Bethlehem; others insisted it was Jerusalem. That night we lay down under olive trees near the town, and three men went ahead into the town. There they found the Armenian monastery. It was indeed Bethlehem. We went to the monastery and they gave us a room for eight people to sleep in and two dusty mats. We laid one mat underneath us, and the other we pulled over us, and thus went to sleep. It was the first time in many, many weeks that we had slept in a room. It was a great kindness to us and we never forgot that. Likewise, we never forgot the British authorities who had given us shelter and food at Hebron.

The next morning someone came and knocked on our door. We were all fast asleep and he had some difficulty rousing us. We were to get up and be ready for the church service. We told him how tired we were and how long we had gone without sleep, and begged to be excused. "We will go with you some other time," we promised. But our hosts were insistent. "This is the rule of the monastery," they replied. We got up and went. The church was very large, and there were several ceremonies and masses going on in different places. We realised that this was the Church of the Nativity, and different churches had a right to use it for their ceremonies. This day was a great feast day. We didn't even know what day of the week it was. We asked a guard where the Armenian church was, and were shown down a flight of steps to a small, narrow place like a cave. There was no space for all of us to go down. I stood near the entrance, and could only hear the voice of the priest. After the ceremony was over, those inside came out, and the next group went down. In the cave was the manger where Jesus had been born. It was in the hands of the Armenians. We understood that we Armenians had the most precious place.

We set off again immediately. We had to get to Jerusalem as soon as possible. It was about an hour's walk, which was a mere stroll for us! But we were gentlemen now, so we hired some trans-port to go to Jerusalem, and went to St James's monastery.

When we got to this monastery, we were seated around a round table and asked many questions: what sort of hardships had we suffered, and how had we escaped? We told the whole story. Then I told them how my brothers had been left in Karak, and they assured me that they would bring all the Armenian refugees from Karak. After this they gave us an *oke* of good bread each, which we took away and ate. There were many refugees in the monastery, and each had a place and a bed. But there was no place for us to sit, and when evening came we had nowhere to sleep. We went to the man in charge of the rooms, who was also the chief priest (*Vartabed*) and asked him for a room. "My sons," he replied, "We have no place free." We begged very hard, but it was no use. So we asked him to give us a blanket each, but he did not have blankets either. This was too much for us, but what could be done? Some of our party slept outside the monastery in a ruined barrack. I had some friends in the monastery, and I managed to shack down with them. The next morning we were given our rations again.

While I was walking in the monastery, I met a gentleman with a walking stick, wearing eyeglasses. He must have been about sixty years old, and was well dressed. He asked me some questions; in particular, where had we slept the night before?

"In the ruins of the barrack," I replied.

He said he was very sorry about that. There were many rooms in the monastery, and many blankets, but the *Vartabed* would not give them to refugees. "We were very angry about this," the gentleman assured me. Naturally, on hearing that there were spare rooms and beds in the monastery, we became rather heated too. Two of our group had been in this monastery before, and they knew their way around. The gentlemen advised us that if we were to give this *Vartabed* a good beating he would soon give us a room to sleep in. He also had some reason to take revenge on the priest. If anybody came from the government to try and arrest us, we were to call him immediately and he would come and translate for us. He would be in the shop near the monastery gate, and would come to us anytime we needed him.

At noon we went again to the *Vartabed*. We asked him for blankets, and with harsh words he again refused to give us any. A little while later an English sergeant came to us with twelve soldiers, all with rifles and bayonets. They came to us and started talking, but we could not understand what was being said. Apparently the *Vartabed* had telephoned for these soldiers to come and arrest us. He had reported us as troublemakers in the monastery. While we were wondering what to say, the gentleman with the walking stick came up and started talking to the soldiers.

He told them we were not creating trouble; there was no murder or bloodshed, it was simply church politics, and with this he succeeded in sending them away. We were feeling braver now. We spent that night in the ruined barracks, too, and the next morning we got our ration again. At that time, we had no idea where the food was coming from; it was, of course, from the Armenian community.

At noon the *Vartabed* called us, and addressed us politely with a smile. "My children, plenty of blankets have come to the station, and tomorrow we can get them for you. Or, if you want them tonight, go down to the station and bring as many as you can carry." I objected to having to go. These people could do anything they liked, and if they wanted, they could soon have the blankets brought today. "We're not porters," I told the *Vartabed*. Of course, he was not too pleased at my words. "In that case, no blankets tonight, either," he replied.

At this, some of our party started arguing for going to bring the blankets. "It's the least we can do for the community. We've done much worse in the past. Let's go and bring some blankets. They are for us, after all." As the majority seemed to be in favour of this, we set off for the station.

As we were walking around the wagons I noticed English soldiers coming out. We thought they were going to give us the blankets. They took two of us to each wagon, opened the door and told us to go in. My friend went in first. "There's no blankets in here!" he cried.

I also peeped in and saw nothing. "Nothing!" I said to the soldiers, in Arabic.

The soldier held my hand and said, "Come on, come on," and pushed me into the wagon. The door was shut behind us, and we realised that we had been taken prisoner, although we had no idea what we were being punished for. There was nobody around to explain our situation to. There was no bread or water, and we wondered how long we were going to be left there. Who could we explain our case to?

All we could hear was the voices of other prisoners in the wagons around us. Some were cursing loudly; others were laughing. In the evening they brought us a load of bread on the back of a mule. Two gentlemen, a lady and a priest came and called to us. When my friends saw these people they got very angry and began to curse at them. Then the visitors gently and kindly replied, "We heard what has happened to you and we came to help and cheer you. Why are you swearing at us?" They gave us bread and money. They were from the Armenian Benevolent Society. We asked them where we were being taken, but they didn't know. "The British army occupied this area only a few days ago," they said, "but they occupied Jerusalem some time ago."

That evening the trains began to move. We had no idea where we were going. At dawn, the train stopped and the wagon doors were opened. An English soldier took us out and we followed him like sheep. He took us to a camp. We passed several tents, and finally he showed us an empty tent, where we would sleep. It was already morning. I saw that there were Armenian refugees coming out of every tent. There were Marash people among them whom I knew. I asked them where we were. They said the place was called Wadi Serar. After a while we were called for; our names were registered and we began to receive regular rations, a bed, a woollen blanket and good food. So once again we had all the comforts of life: meat, white bread, warm bed, comfort and good luck, and, of course, our friends, the lice, but we had got thoroughly used to them by now! The women and children whom we had parted from at Khalil Rahman also came to Wadi Serar.

About Wadi Serar

In the Bible Wadi Serar is called the Valley of Sorek, where Samson burnt the cornfields of the Philistines. It is a wide, open plain, with no towns or villages nearby. There was work for everyone there, similar to the work of the porters in the station. We were rolling hay bales down from the wagons and taking them to the horses, and bags of food to the staff. Everybody was obliged to work. As wages, we would get six *piastres* a day, as well as our food.

This was the central place for transportation. All the refugees of Arabia were being sent here, and from here to the Armenian refugee camp in Port Said. There was transportation every week.

We worked here for about three weeks. I made some money, and wanted to go on to Port Said, and from there to go to Cairo and find work there. The day for transportation came. Names were continually being registered. About one hundred men were transported per week, and the same number of women. I heard that they were short of names to fill the list. Immediately I went to them and my name was added.

The next day we left for Port Said by train. After passing many stations, including Ramlah, we finally reached Kantara. We got off the train. Men and women were separated, and sent to different tents. There were thousands of tents, all surrounded by barbed wire. An English sergeant came and took us to an open sand field. There was a wooden room there. We went in and were instructed to take all our clothes off, until we were completely naked. Our clothes were put in bundles and taken away to steam. Not so much as a handkerchief was left with us. There we remained, naked under the scorching sun. We could not sit down, because the sand was so hot. Finally, two hours later, our clothes were brought back to us. We dressed and came back to the camp, where we saw a huge bath filled with chemical water. Everybody was obliged to go into the bath and dip themselves in the water. One by one we filed in. The chemical water was so strong it burned our bodies, especially the places where we were scratched from the lice. One by one we came out of the bath screaming, and dashed around the camp as if there was fire coming out of every single hair on our head. This lasted only for ten minutes or so. Once we were cool again we put on our clothes.

We stayed there for another two days. Again, food was rationed to us. But finally, once and for all, we were free from our lice-companions! After two days an Armenian officer came in a French uniform, bringing a civilian Armenian with him. He was the interpreter for the French Army. He advised us to join the Armenian Volunteer Force. Some people signed up. He had a great propaganda system, reminding us all about how the Turks had massacred our nation, and saying that now we had the opportunity to join the Volunteer Force and take our revenge. Once his propaganda was finished every Armenian felt obliged to join up. I thought about my own plans. If I went to Egypt, I would have no money, and I had no contacts there. So I joined the force too. If I survived the war, all well and good, but if I was killed, well, I was as good as dead in my present lifestyle anyway; at least I would die as a volunteer fighting to avenge my nation.

The next day they returned. I was taken to the doctor for an examination. There was a French captain, the doctor and a French Army priest there. When they saw me, they thought I was too young to join the Army, and generally too weak. "You are not fit enough," they informed me. I insisted that I was 20 years old. But they still objected. "You are too weak, you will never be able to carry the army bag," they said.

"That is because I have been walking through the mountains for over a month, and I am weakened. When I join the army, I will be all right," I insisted. They were eventually persuaded to enlist me. The doctor said my general health was all right. They sent me off, telling me they would call me again later.

I was quite happy at the idea of having become a soldier, but on the other hand I kept thinking about my brothers. One of them was fifteen and the other was ten. Who would look after them? We were sent away from Kantara to the camp at Port Said. This camp was on the other side of the Suez Canal, on a sandy field. The Suez was between the camp and Port Said. There were thousands of tents there. Armenians from Mousa Dagh (Svedia) were also at this camp. Several books have been written about this camp and the Svedian people. These Mousa Dagh Armenians had held out against the Turks for forty days, and French warships had gone to bring them to Port Said. All the details of this interesting history are recorded in the book *The Forty Days of Musa Dagh*.

We stayed in the Port Said camp for a few days, and then all those who had enlisted were taken to the army camp at Port Said. We began to eat army bread. The next day we were given army uniforms. It was July 2, 1917, and we were enlisted as French soldiers.

About Volunteer Life

At Port Said we began army exercises and disciplines. Eight days later two boats transported us out of Port Said towards Cyprus, about a six-hour passage. However, our boat sighted a German submarine, and, signalling to the other boat, we turned back again to Port Said. Next morning when we landed back in Port Said we all took steamboats and went to the Armenian refugee camp. That night in the army camp, when they found all our tents empty, they telephoned the commander of the refugee camp to arrest all the soldiers and send them immediately back to the army camp. The camp policemen searched the camp and took all of us, separating men from their families. We went back to the shore of the canal, but there was no steamboat on which to cross. So we waited there till morning, talking and laughing. In the morning the boats came and we went back to our tents. We were reprimanded and told that once we had arrived in Cyprus we would be grounded for three days.

The next day we set sail again for Cyprus in two boats and a small warship. We arrived at the town of Boghaz on the coast of Cyprus. As soon as the boats anchored German planes appeared. They tried to bomb the boats, but the boats manoeuvred. We disembarked and made our way to the army camp.

After we had had three days of rest, they examined us, divided us into groups and gave us all numbers. My number was 3983.

We began to do serious training. The first two battalions were full, but the third battalion needed a hundred men to complete it. Every battalion consisted of about one thousand soldiers.

For 15 days our gruelling exercises continued, but we tired of the food long before. Every noon we were fed ladies fingers (okra) and for supper, egg-plant (aubergine).

One evening, just before bedtime, as we sat around chatting and joking, I commented, "We've been here fifteen days now, and we've seen nothing but egg-plant and ladies fingers. How long is this going to go on for?"

Among us there were corporals from the 1st Battalion, who were our trainers, and spoke French. All our sergeants were French; only the corporals were Armenian. These corporals told us that the 1st and 2nd Battalions got very nice food. "Why are they feeding you like that?" they puzzled. "If I were you, I would object!"

So we decided that the next morning when we went out for our training, instead of counting as usual, we would say "*Bamya, Batljan*" (okra and aubergine). About 200 of us agreed to repeat these words. We asked the more experienced corporals what we should do if they decided to punish us. They said that if five or six of us were taken to prison, all two hundred soldiers should go to prison with them, and there is no rule that allows all the soldiers to be put into prison!

The following morning a French sergeant was commanding us. After a few commands he ordered us to start counting, as usual. From the first soldier to the last we started "*Bamya, Batljan, Bamya, Batljan.*"

The sergeant stopped us. "What's the matter with you all?" he cried. "You've counted all right every day. What's all this funny counting today?"

Again, he ordered us to count, and again, the same chant began: "*Bamya, Batljan.*"

By this time the sergeant was getting very angry. He stopped us and started us a third time, and at the third chant of "*Bamya, Batljan*" he got quite hot under the collar. He asked the corporals what was going on, to which they primly replied they did not know. So he marched off to tell the commander, and the commander came to inspect us!

This time, the commander ordered us to count. Again, we began our chant: "*Bamya, Batljan.*" He was most surprised, and not a little angry.

"What do they mean by this?" he asked, and again he ordered us to count, and again we repeated "*Bamya, Batljan.*"

So the commander called out ten men, and on the command "Right turn, quick march" we set off for interrogation. After a few steps, all the soldiers came after us. The commander tried to stop them, but they said that if we were guilty, then they were all guilty. Why were only ten of them being taken prisoners?

Seeing that he couldn't stop them, the commander turned round and began to reason. "What do you mean by all this?" Now that was exactly the question we were waiting for.

"Ever since we got here," we replied, "we've been fed *Batljan* at noon and *Bamya* in the evening. We are sick of them, and we can't eat them any more. We have no strength left to do exercises, learn anything new, or anything!"

The commander was astonished. "There must be a misunderstanding," he assured us. "Be patient today, and tomorrow I will make sure your diet is changed."

Then he commanded us, "Turn about!" and soon the command to count came, and – lo and behold – we all suddenly remembered how to count correctly.

"*Bon*," said the commander, and the exercises continued with no further interruptions that day.

The next day we had hot rice, soup and a cup of wine for lunch. After that the food got better; we even had meat in our diet.

Training and exercise continued every day. One day of the week we were issued with a brush and piece of soap. That was wash day. We and our clothes were given a good scrubbing. The exercises were mostly on foot, with bayonets, and various war manoeuvres. Once a week we had shooting practice. I was good at shooting and would sometimes win a prize, usually a packet of cigarettes.

We stayed in Cyprus for about three and a half months, progressing steadily with the army exercises. Then they separated off a group of us who had done well in the training and we were sent on to relieve regular soldiers. About two hundred from our company were sent to Kastellorizo Island, where we replaced another company of two hundred, who were sent to complete the 3rd Battalion.

Kastellorizo was a small island on the side of a mountain, close to Turkey. The majority of its inhabitants were Greeks, and about a quarter of them were Turks. We could see houses and villages in Turkey from the island. At night time, when standing at the nearest spot, we could even hear the voices from Turkey.

There was no water on the island. A few rain water reservoirs had been made to see us through the winter. There were no vegetables or greenery on the island, and no farming. The only work was for fishermen and sponge collectors, who worked on the sea. Their trade was with Turkey and Rhodes. The population of the island was only a few thousand. The Turks had left and escaped to Turkey, and the soldiers took up residence in the Turkish houses.

We were on this island for about four months. An order came for us to prepare to join the Nablus battle front, which we were very happy about. At last, the chance to fight! We were eagerly awaiting the second order, when a cable came saying that Germany had surrendered. Of course, there was a great celebration on receiving this news. We were shooting and shouting and celebrating in our own way, when we heard that our ammunition store was on fire and had exploded. The building was destroyed. The next day about twenty soldiers were sent to clear the ruins. There were many bombs and other ammunition that had not yet gone off. They needed to be taken out of the debris. It was a very dangerous job.

We all worked there in turn. French sailors had also arrived on the island and they worked with us. One bomb exploded, ripping one soldier's leg off and killing another. But eventually the job was finished. A few days after news of the German surrender came a report that the Turks had also surrendered. Of course, there was more celebration on our island. Then our captain and a translator crossed over to Turkey in a steamboat, waving a white flag. The Turks arrested them and asked questions. The captain replied that Turkey had surrendered, and he had come to accept their congratulations. The Turks blindfolded him and took him to the Turkish commander. There his blindfold was removed and they shook hands together. The commander told our captain that he had heard of no such surrender. So they sent our captain back, but en route he had permission to do some trading in Turkey, and he brought back with him a bullock, a basket of eggs and a few chickens.

That evening he told us about his meeting with the Turkish commander, and that they were not yet aware of the armistice. So we continued the blackout and kept guards on the shores. One day the army ship came and we were ready to land in Turkey, not with rifles, but with sticks. We went into the boat, and about 200 Armenian soldiers set sail from Kastellorizo bound for Alexandretta.

Occupation of Alexandretta

When our ship pulled in at Alexandretta, we found that some English and French officers with some Algerian soldiers had already occupied Alexandretta. Nevertheless, we were the first army force to land in Alexandretta. I was the first to disembark. The people of Alexandretta came to watch us land. We were talking in Armenian with each other. A tall man with a red fez on his head, rather skinny, was following us. He could see that we were foreigners, but he couldn't work out what nationality we were. We scared him away, but he came near us again, so we pointed the rifle at him, and that made him disappear for a while. By now, a number of Armenian soldiers had disembarked, and the man heard us talking Armenian together, and plucking up his courage he came again, and as we were waving him away he cried in Armenian, "Are you Armenians?" and we replied, "Yes!"

"Where are you coming from?" he called. At first he had thought we were Turkish soldiers.

"We are the French Volunteer soldiers," we told him.

"How many Armenians are there among you?"

"We are all Armenians. Only the captain and some officers are French. From now on these countries are no longer under Turkish rule, but French rule."

The man looked at all the young soldiers and nearly danced for joy. Then he rushed away to tell the other Armenians; apparently there were a few Armenian houses nearby. So they all came from the other side of town to the soldiers' barracks to see us.

Meanwhile, the captain had formed us into lines and with swords in hand and bayonets fixed on rifles we marched into the market place. In the very centre of the market he commanded us to halt. Of course, this was just a show for the benefit of the Turks, and one could tell they didn't like it a bit. In fact, the only Turks to be seen were those who were escaping. First we were commanded to march with our arms on our shoulders, and then he commanded us to sing our Armenian song, "We are the Armenian Volunteer Soldiers." We were singing and marching and stamping our feet loudly on the ground. When we came near the barracks, we found the Armenian men, women and children gathered round, weeping and throwing flowers and fragrances over us, until we had all returned to our barracks. Only some time later did the crowd disperse and everyone go home.

After a while, Algerian soldiers came and relieved us. We began to march to Kirik Khan. When we arrived in Beylan we settled down in a garden near a valley for lunch, and the Armenians in Beylan heard that Armenian soldiers were passing through the town. As we marched through the market we saw all the Armenians lining both sides of the market. They had stood there for two hours waiting for us. As we passed there were loud cries of "*Getse Hayer!*" "Long live the Armenians!" There was much commotion, clapping and shouting and other expressions of joy. We marched on and arrived at Kirik Khan. We set up headquarters in Kirik Khan, and from there, twelve were sent to Top Baghaz, twelve to Mourad Pasha, and about forty of us to Hamam. I was among the forty. We were in charge of the villages in the Hamam district. This was an area between Aleppo and Alexandretta. The villagers were very much afraid of us. If we heard of any trouble in the villages, we would get ten or twelve horses from the village, ride to the trouble spot and arrest the chief and the *mukhtar* of the village, and bring them to our captain at Kirik Khan.

There was a hot mineral spring in Hamam where the sick would bathe. In fact, the name *Hamam* means "bath" in Turkish. We used to bathe in this spring every day, and spend many a pleasant time there. Still, my mind was restless on account of my brothers. My mates would comfort me, saying, "Think what a grand party we'll have when you hear that your brothers have arrived safe and sound in Port Said or in the camp in Jerusalem!"

One day, the mail arrived. They were reading out the names in front of the barrack doors, and everybody was getting letters from their loved ones. I kept thinking of my brothers, and the tears came unbidden. I wondered where they were. Maybe one day I would get a letter from them. As the thought passed my mind, I heard my name being called. I rushed down, nearly tumbling down the steps in my eagerness, and took the letter. "Timoteos and Sarkis have arrived in safety, and your elder brother Yervant is in Damascus. We have received a letter from him, too, and he is well. Signed, H Simonian." I knew Simonian. Before I joined the army in the Port Said camp he had been the deputy in charge of the tents. He was also a relative of ours. I had given him my address and asked him to write to me if ever my brothers arrived in Port Said. As I read the note my sorrow was turned to tears of joy. I praised God for this. Then my mates reminded me of the party we were supposed to have on this occasion, and I was more than willing to comply. As it was, our daily life felt like one long party. But we received only fifteen francs a month, which was not enough for our coffee and cigarettes.

One day we were sitting or lying around on the grass in front of our barracks, chatting. The sun was shining warmly. I noticed a caravan of camels moving in our direction. We got up and went forward to inspect them.

After inspection, we allowed them to continue their journey, and we came back to our places and continued lying around talking. Then I noticed a Kurdish child coming towards us. We threw a stone at him to frighten him off. He ran away, and stood staring at us from a safe distance. Then he started coming towards us again. One of our mates began to swear at him in Kurdish and drove him off. Half an hour later he was back again. We thought maybe he was hungry, so our friend, who spoke Kurdish, asked him what he wanted. The child was trying to hear what language we were speaking. Then he spoke to us in Armenian. "Are you Armenians?"

"Yes," we replied, "we are Armenians." Then we embraced the child, and he threw his red hat off his head. Immediately long golden tresses tumbled down, and we realised "he" was a young girl, about 13 or 14 years old. She was a real beauty.

The young girl's story was an unusual one. When Armenian refugees had been passing through the villages of Kilis, one of the Kurdish chiefs took this girl; whether she had been left behind en route or stolen from her family we never found out. The chief was keeping her to give to his son when she grew up. Then one day when she was playing with the Kurdish children she heard that there were Armenian soldiers in Hamam. Suddenly her patriotic blood started tingling in her veins and she decided to leave the Kurds and come and find us. So one day she dressed herself up like a boy, took a little bread with her, and began to walk. On the way, she met some Kurdish men with their camels. They asked her where she was going, and she said, "The chief of Haman is my relative. I am going to him." So they gave her a lift to Haman, where she left them and came and found us.

The girl stayed with us a few days, and we fed her, made dresses for her, gave her some money and, according to her wishes, sent her on to Alexandretta, to a workhouse, where several Armenians were living and working. The house was for Armenians with no relatives or no-one to look after them. If any living relatives were later found, they were sent on to them.

One day some trouble arose in Kilis village, about three hours away from us. A report of it was brought to our captain, who ordered us to go and arrest the *mukhtar* of the village and bring him to him. About twelve Armenian soldiers and an Armenian sergeant went. We got twelve horses from near the village and rode into the village. There was some sort of a feast going on, with music and drums. When they saw us they stopped the music and commotion.

We had no desire to disturb their joy, so we said nothing of our mission. They killed a sheep for us and prepared food. We were entertained in the *mukhtar*'s house. We asked where the *mukhtar* himself was, and were told he had gone to Aleppo!

We had heard previously that there was an Armenian girl in that village. We went to the house where she was living and found her there. So we told her to pack her things and come with us, but she refused. However hard we begged her to allow us to save her from the Kurds, she would not come. We kept telling her we would send her to her parents and that she had nothing to fear if she would just come with us. Eventually, we tried to take her by force, but nothing worked. She said she had a Kurdish husband and children and vowed that she would rather die than leave them. "My parents died and these people are my parents now," she said. By now, we were already late and we had to go back. We left her there and went back to the *mukhtar*'s house. The lamb was ready by now and we had a real feast. Then we took the *mukhtar*'s son in lieu of the *mukhtar* and rode back to Hamam. At night the *mukhtar* came with some other men. We let the son go free and sent the *mukhtar* to Kirik Khan.

Armenian Fighters Come to Visit

One day, the captain received a cable from the British authorities in Aleppo, saying that the Armenian insurgents who lived on the Giavour Dagh Mountains during the war were coming from Aleppo on their way to Adana. They would be passing through Kirik Khan, where they must be welcomed and given accommodation.

They were about forty men, who had run away from the Armenian massacres and deportations in different areas and had gathered in the Giavour Dagh Mountains. For three years they had fought against the Turks from there, until the war ended. Many

Turkish troops had attacked them, but all who attacked them were destroyed. They used to raid villages for food and other spoils, and return to their mountains. There was also a woman from Zeytoun among them. When the war ended they went to Aleppo and surrendered their arms to the English general, who sent them to Adana. They came on foot to Kirik Khan, where they stayed one night. The next morning they set off for Adana via Alexandretta.

Their chief did not want to surrender his arms to the English. About five of the men came walking through the mountains and came to Kirik Khan, where they stayed in an inn. We heard about their coming, and three of us – two from Marash and one from Zeytoun – went to see them to hear what news they had from our people. They were very pleased to see us. Their clothes were made of leather and their bodies were lined with cartridges. They each carried a German rifle and a bayonet at their waist. Their coats were also of leather, especially designed for carrying cartridges. There were rows of cartridges on their legs from their knees upwards, and cartridges all across their breasts.

We told them which road they should be taking, and where the Volunteer Corps station was situated. They thanked us, but said, "We go through the mountains, not along the road." It was already evening, and they prepared to set out to Adana through the mountains. We returned to our barracks.

Return to Alexandretta

There were some Armenian Volunteer soldiers of the 4th Battalion in Alexandretta, but having only recently joined the army they were inexperienced in army discipline. They caused some trouble in Alexandretta and were banished to Port Said as punishment, where they were kept behind barbed wire. We were sent to Alexandretta to take their posts, and Senegalese soldiers were sent to take our place. We heard that a couple of days later the villagers had shot two Senegalese soldiers.

In Alexandretta we were called in to the army office. We were commanded to leave our rifles in one room, our cartridges in another and our bags in the next room and then to leave by the back door and return to the barracks. We were all angry at having our arms taken away without any notice.

They sent us from there to Beirut, and a month later, on a particularly rough and stormy day, they sent us to Port Said in a great French battleship. Those who wished to stay in Alexandretta as civilians were allowed to do so. After another month in Port Said, on June 17, 1919 our uniforms were also taken and we were issued with a civilian suit of some very cheap material, like prisoners' clothing. From there we were sent penniless to the Port Said refugee camp. There, at long last, I was reunited with my younger brothers.

Chapter 7

Reunited and Still on the Move

Civilian Life Once More

There were thousands of refugees living in tents in the Port Said camp. I was given a tent with my brothers, and a meal three times a day, which was brought to our tents. The camp was under British rule. There was no forced labour, and we all enjoyed a good holiday! There were, however, odd jobs to do if you wanted to earn a little extra pocket money. The tents were all kept spotlessly clean. There were special monitors appointed to go around checking the tents. There was free food and water, and in this conducive atmosphere several marriages took place. The government gave special aid to the newlyweds.

One day we heard that in Cairo they were giving twelve Egyptian pounds to those who had been in the Armenian Volunteer Force. The French Army used to keep a record of our monthly pay, which we would receive on leaving the army. This money was then given to our National Union Committee in Egypt, but we never saw it.

When we heard this news, 20 to 30 ex-volunteer soldiers gathered together and found some old uniforms. We took our certificates, and clad in the old uniforms we went down to the Port Said

station and showed the Arab Egyptian policemen our certificates.
They thought we must be on leave. From there we took the train to
Cairo. We saw many Turkish prison camps from the train windows
as we passed by. In Cairo our National Committee gave us accommodation in the school building. We went to the Armenian
Committee leaders and laid our case before them. They refused to
give us anything. We stayed there for about a month, demanding
our money, and eventually we received six Egyptian pounds each.
We took the money and returned to our camp. I bought some second-hand clothes, some for myself and some to sell for more money.
This was pretty good business, but once we were back in camp and
no longer had our uniforms we were not able to get out of the camp
again. That money soon finished.

Then we heard that the rest of the money had been given to
ex-service men in Alexandria. This time twelve of us found some
uniforms and set out for Alexandria. Again, we were given accommodation in a school building. We stayed there for a month, and
after considerable difficulty we finally received the rest of our wage,
six Egyptian pounds. It was as if they were giving us charity.

During our stay in Alexandria we heard that Nouri Chavoush of
Tafilah, the man who used to tell us Armenians, "I am your God",
was in the prison camp of Alexandria. Once a week he had permission to come to a coffee house on the beach. We all wanted him to
see us in our uniforms, and we went to the coffee house several
times, but he never came. He had heard that some Tafilah refugees
were in Alexandria in uniform, and were looking for him, and he
was too afraid to come to town. We never saw him. On the way
back to Port Said I bought second-hand clothes again and sold them
in the camp. But I could not obtain permission to go again and buy
more.

The first time I went to Cairo I found a job for myself, and
could have stayed there. But at this time one of my brothers had a
problem with his eye, and the other was still very young. I couldn't

leave them. I thought instead about taking them with me to Aleppo and from there, with my elder brother, I would go back to Marash. There, I thought, we had a chance to marry and settle down and begin our life again. With this in mind I gave up the idea of working in Cairo and tried to find some odd jobs in the camp at Port Said.

I had a close friend at the camp, and together we used to go to Port Said by the "unofficial" route. We would buy vegetables and dates to sell in the camp. There was an official camp harbour, and shopkeepers had permission to bring things there and sell them. We also went to buy and sell things "unofficially". The boatman, knowing that we were breaking rules, always demanded more money from us, which sometimes we would pay, and sometimes we would not. If we did not, there was always a fight instead. But the business soon stopped; people were afraid to buy in secret, and we were afraid to carry on.

So we hired a shop instead and began grocery work, which we did for some time. Then one day I received a letter from my elder brother in Aleppo, saying, "I am returning to Marash. All the Marash people are going back. But I don't want to go alone. Come back and let's all four of us go back together and rebuild our ancestral home."

I decided to take my brothers and go. In any case, the atmosphere in the camp was beginning to get very unhealthy. People had formed themselves into "Huntchag, "Tashnag" and "National Liberty" parties, and there were a lot of skirmishes. Since I had a lot of relatives in the camp I began to get dragged into their quarrels.

Then an order came for everyone in the camp to prepare to return to their own country. We started by train from Port Said to Kantara, and from Kantara to Haifa, where we stayed the night. Five days later we arrived in Aleppo on a Sunday morning. In Aleppo they took us to the Citadel, which was now the centre for transportation. From there everyone was being sent to his own country. I thought to myself that my elder brother always went to church on Sunday morning, and I would be able to find him there. So I went with some friends to the Armenian church in the city. A few minutes later my brother walked in. After a joyful reunion we proceeded together to the Citadel to see Timoteos and Sarkis.

We decided to hire a place in Aleppo, so that my brother could arrange his affairs there, and then we would return to our own country, to Marash. Others went on to Marash, but we hired a place and remained in Aleppo for about three months. We took Timoteos to a doctor there, but the news was bad. There was no hope for one eye and the other needed an immediate operation. The bad eye had to be removed, so that the remaining eye would strengthen, otherwise the other eye would also be affected. So we took him to the hospital, where one eye was removed and the other operated on.

During this time, we noticed that Armenians were coming from Marash and buying rifles and arms. The Turks were also coming to buy rifles and arms. Although the place was under French rule, we noticed that the situation grew worse daily. We decided not to go to Marash, and remained in Aleppo.

One day we received a letter from my uncle Mr Hampartsum Pambakian in Tarsus; we did not know him or he us, as he had moved to Tarsus before we were born, but he wrote the following words to us:

"My dear nephews, as you are not able to return to your own country, come to Tarsus, and let's meet."

On reflection, this did not appear a bad course to choose. I took Sarkis to Tarsus, and Timoteos stayed in Aleppo with Yervant. Yervant had good work there as a tailor, but he said to me, "See if tailor's work is good in Tarsus, and if it is, write to me and I'll come, too."

So for the time being we parted. Sarkis and I took a train and then a boat, and we went to my uncle's shop. It was 1920.

Life in Tarsus

My uncle in Tarsus had a good business and a large blacksmith's shop. One side of the shop was a melting house. He took us to his home, where we met my aunt and another nephew who was living with them. There my aunt cooked and cared for us and loved us like a mother.

My uncle asked me what work I did. I replied that I was a tailor, but he shook his head sadly. "Tailor's work will not bring in money now," he said. "You can work here in my shop at the melting work." I accepted gladly, and worked there for three months. I also wrote to Yervant, telling him to come to Tarsus.

But at this time the French army and all the officers left Marash secretly during the night without giving any notice, or warning the Armenians of the coming danger. When the Armenians heard the commotion at night, many of them woke up and began to run away after them. The French had persuaded the Armenians to fight against the Turks in Marash, and now they were escaping secretly and leaving the Armenians to their fate! Armenian soldiers, men, women and children all followed them; about 8,000 of them were on their way to Adana. A heavy snowstorm started on the way and many were frozen to death. Parents were forced to abandon their children en route and some children forced to leave behind frozen parents. Of those who made it to Tarsus, many lost their fingers and some even their legs to frostbite. The story of these journeys can be read in detail in *The History of Marash*, where all the facts were carefully recorded. I saw the Marash people when they arrived in Tarsus. One of them was a relative of mine.

Then my brothers Yervant and Timoteos also came to Tarsus. And about this time Turkish brigands became active around the town. I was going to my uncle's vineyards, supervising workmen there. It was a dangerous life. Many were being attacked on the mountains by the brigands. One day I went to the vineyard on horseback. I took a revolver with me. There were Turkish and Kurdish labourers in our vineyard. Some of the labourers came up to me and said, "Master, if I hit you on the head with this axe, what good would your revolver be?"

"If I was afraid I would not have come here," I replied boldly.

"Oh, don't listen to him, he's a fool," others muttered.

But I understood the situation. At noon I ate by myself near my horse. Toward the evening I heard the sound of gunshots. Immediately I jumped on my horse and began to ride back to Tarsus. I saw two *jandarmas* coming after me on horseback. There was a little village further on that the brigands had taken. In any case, all the inhabitants were Turkish, and of the same mind as the brigands. I arrived to find Tarsus surrounded by Turks.

The Battle of the Brigands in Tarsus

There were some French soldiers in Tarsus, but very few. They turned to the Armenians for help.

"We don't have enough manpower," they told us. "We'll give you arms and ammunition if you help us."

The Armenian community was disturbed by this turn of events. At first they were reluctant to fight, but the French forced their hand. Everybody was armed. Any Armenian you saw in the street had firearms and cartridges. There was even some shooting in the streets. I didn't want to join in, but I received a letter from the leaders of our community saying, "Our people need an experienced man like yourself. You know how to handle firearms. Why are you shying away? Come and join the fight." What could I do? Again, I thought of my nation and picked up my rifle.

They gave me twelve men to train in the use of firearms. First we began to make trenches between the Armenian and Turkish quarters. There was a Turkish abbey (*tekke*) in our quarter, and two orphans were living in it. We tried to send them away to their own people, but one of them refused to go. We left him there, but took the abbey, and the authorities left it under my control! We were to guard the street corner called Tahta-Mezar ("Wooden Tomb"). Then we moved to the garden of Keor Oghlan. By this time there was a serious food shortage in Tarsus.

The French soldiers used to go to the Turkish houses in the Armenian quarters, taking some Armenians with them, to break in and rob goods such as carpets, or other precious goods. They would give the important spoils to the Armenians they had taken with them. An order came from the commander forbidding Armenians to break into Turkish houses and rob them. By this time a lot of the spoils had reached France in safety and others had found their way to his own house.

By now the Turks of Tarsus had left their homes and fled into the mountains. There were very few Turks left in the town. Had the Armenians wanted to rob them, there was a golden opportunity now to plunder many homes. But they did not.

The Turks were still encircling Tarsus. One day we heard that they had raided Isgelig village and were burning it. The inhabitants of that village were Greeks. As the village was quite close to the town the villagers managed to run to the town for safety. The following morning we received an order from the French officers to go to the village and chase the brigands away.

The following morning we all gathered in the church where the priest, after various admonitions and blessings, gave us Holy Communion. There were Greeks with us, too. While we were still in the church an Arab boy came riding up on horseback. "Come quickly," he called, "The Turks have come to Mousalla!" The Mousalla district was all gardens, and was attached to Tarsus. If once the Turks entered that district it would be difficult to chase them away.

So we rushed down to Mousalla, to defend this key position. We were about 150 men, fully armed. As we entered the furthest part of the gardens they saw us. They were using an old flour mill (the Sorsofan factory) as their base. Its three back windows were overlooking our advance. At one of these windows they had placed a German machine gun, and as we advanced, they began to fire at us. Immediately the sergeants ordered us to lie down on the ground. Slowly we crept forward to the other end of the garden, from where we began our defence. Noon came and went and still both sides were firing at each other over the open gardens. Cries of "Keep on firing" and volleys of shots filled the air. Then we saw some of the brigands coming upwards and behind, to surround us. Immediately men were sent to check their advance.

Others ran back to Tarsus and spread the evil tidings that the Armenian fighters had been surrounded by the Turkish brigands. Immediately there was a hue and cry, and panic spread, as the residents began tearfully to fear the worst. But on the fields we kept up the shooting. We saw the Turks coming down the steps of the mill and we opened fire on them. One of our own men was shot in the chest. We sent him back to Tarsus, but he died en route.

When evening had almost come we saw smoke coming from the factory. We wondered at the Turks calmly making their supper! Then we realised that the factory was on fire. Also, we noticed that the noise of the machine gun had stopped. They were burning the factory and evacuating. Suddenly we all remembered how hungry we were! But there was no food to be had. All those who were left gathered together, but we saw that at least 60 of our men had run away. If we left too, the brigands would return and all our efforts would be in vain, so we decided to remain. As time slowly passed we became more and more hungry and increasingly angry. At 1 a.m. we saw a carriage coming. Immediately I jumped up and with a few men went down the road to meet it and ordered the driver to halt.

"Who are you?" I asked.

"The servant of God," came the reply.

"Where are you coming from?"

"I have travelled far."

"Hands up," I cried, taken aback by his replies. "Hands up or I'll shoot."

His hands shot up. "What do you have in the carriage?" I continued, and immediately went to investigate for myself. I found two full bags.

"What are these?" I asked.

"Bread."

I opened them. He was speaking the truth. "Where are you from?" I asked.

"From Tarsus."

Now I understood what had happened. I quietly spoke the password and immediately he replied correctly. He was bringing bread to us from Mr Shalvardjian's flour factory. We took the bread and divided it among ourselves. It would last us until the morning.

All night we heard the voices of women and children from a village close by. In the morning, we heard that that village had been evacuated during the night, and we received a message from the French to go and burn the village. In two hours they were going to start cannon fire in those districts. We hurried to the village and burnt it down, but the French never opened fire. We saw many bloodied rags lying around the village.

Exhausted, we arrived back at Tarsus. I was covered in dust and muck and perspiration. I rested for the rest of the day, but by the next I was burning with fever. The rest of our men went to burn some other villages by order of the French. The villages were about fifteen minutes from each other. Our men passed the first village, which we had burnt the previous day, but as they approached the second village the brigands came up from behind and the two opposing groups got mixed up, as both groups had the same uniform. As they were unable to tell who was friend and who was foe, no-one dared open fire! There were Greeks, Arabs, Turks and Armenians there. The Tarsus-dwellers all ran away, but the brigands remained. About twelve of our men, against orders, went on to burn the third village, and of the twelve, eleven were taken prisoner. One of them escaped into the bushes and after hiding there for two days came safely back to Tarsus.

After that, we would go out of town to fight the Turks for 24 hour shifts and then return to town to rest for 24 hours. We slept between the Turkish and Armenian quarters. During the 24 hours in town I would be able to go home just long enough to take off my boots, change my socks, and then head back to my posts. For three months I slept with my clothes and boots on, and fully armed. We were backwards and forwards between the town and the surrounding villages, alternating between open conflict and uneasy ceasefires.

In the morning the brigands would disappear, only to come close again at night. They were farmers during the day, and we could see them chasing after their oxen. But at night they would become brigands. I remember seeing one chasing his ox in the day and being shot down dead that night. These brigands had set a guard near us. Regularly, every fifteen minutes, he would shoot into the air, until we were all quite tired of the noise. A number of us had searched in vain for his guard post, until one day one of our men who was surveying the area with binoculars saw him. In the middle of a large field there were three trees, and in one of these he had made a wooden bed, where he used to sleep, perched up in the tree like a bird. Quickly my friend called me over, crying, "Corporal, corporal, bring me my rifle!"

I knew he must have seen the guard, and running over I picked up the binoculars and looked for myself. Taking the rifle into my own hands I succeeded in removing the irritation of his presence from the guard post! His body remained under the tree for many days. No one dared come and take it away. We knew that our position was very dangerous and our life hung on a thread. Of course, the essence of war is to kill or be killed. We knew the same could happen to us any day.

On day we were ordered to go and meet a column of French soldiers coming from Adana. They had been attacked en route by a party of Turks and in the ensuing fight, in which the Turks had come out worse, the French had taken 200 Turkish prisoners.

The column went on to the Mersina Mountains, where they were pursuing the brigands. We were ordered to wait at the foot of the mountains on the opposite side to catch any escaping brigands.

We set off early the next morning. The place we had been sent to was not far behind the station. But it was an unsatisfactory position, and our leader was quite inexperienced. He ordered twenty of us to wait at the white rock at the back, and the rest marched forward toward the brigands.

I looked at the place he had pointed out. There was nowhere to defend oneself, and we had brought no tools with us to make defences. There was nothing but a cotton field between us and the brigands. Thirty men were walking through the cotton fields. At the back, we were tying white ribbons or handkerchiefs on our arms, so that if we mixed with the brigands we would be able to tell friend from foe, because we were all dressed like civilians. I did not like our position, but I didn't dare tell our leader. I confided in another friend, also a corporal. "Tie those ribbons on slowly. Don't rush! I'm in no hurry! This is jolly dangerous. We shouldn't advance. But there's no point telling the sergeant, he won't listen."

We kicked our heels and dragged the job out, despite the sergeant's attempts to rush us. Eventually, he sent out the thirty men with their corporal. Before they reached their appointed place the brigands saw them and opened fire. Immediately they fell flat on their faces. We got down onto the road, which was four or five feet below the field. The brigands obviously could not see us well. Had they been able to see us, there would have been no survivors from the group that had gone ahead into the field. As it was, they lay there, unable either to attack or to retreat. The sun beat mercilessly on us, and we had no food or water. With bullets flying continually over our heads, we dared not even move. Finally the sergeant ordered two of us to go to the people in front and tell them to escape. But with bullets raining all around us, it was not easy for him to find even two volunteers! I noticed that he was trying to send some by force.

"You can't force them to go down!" I objected. "Everybody's life is precious to him. You and I had better go down there together!"

"I can't go!" he argued. "Who's going to look after things here?"

"Well, there's no need, as far as I can see. The danger is there, not here!"

Seeing that there was no decent way of backing out, he set his teeth and growled, "Come on then, let's go."

We went a little further on, where the road was slightly higher. I crawled up first and lay flat in the field. But the sergeant couldn't even lift his head up. Of course, he had a right to be afraid. The machine gun was singing loudly and the shower of bullets continued. I urged him to come up, but in vain. In the end, I jumped down again and we went back to the others.

"What do we do now?" asked the sergeant.

"There's only one thing we can do," I replied. "We must send some of our men up the road, and some to the middle, and some down the other way. We'll open fire on them, and once we've drawn the attack on to ourselves, we'll give our boys a chance to get away under cover."

No-one could suggest anything else, so we immediately put my plan into action. Soon our boys in the field were able to stagger back to us. They were in a miserable condition. Some were wounded. Others fainted as soon as they arrived. Only one was shot down in the escape, and another one had obviously lost his mind under the terrible conditions he had been forced to suffer, and instead of running back to us ran on toward the brigands and was never seen again. We carried the body of the one who had died and buried him in Tarsus. Thus we all went back with only two losses, but rumour had already reached the town that we were all taken prisoner.

Then the French opened the way from Tarsus to Mersin. The train began to work. My brother Yervant went to Mersin and found work there as a tailor. The brigands were cleared from around Tarsus and the surrounding neighbourhood. I handed my arms in to the French officers and followed Yervant to Mersin, where I started working as a tailor. We stayed there for some time, and eventually came back together to Tarsus, and worked there.

At this time my brother Yervant married Isa, the tailor's daughter, and began to work with his father-in-law. I worked in Mr Sarkis of Feke's tailor's shop. He had a good business and he grew to trust me. One day he hired a shop and told me to clean it up and put up shelves in it, and that we would go into business together there as partners. Of course, this was a great opportunity for me. I had no money to start a business on my own. The shop was very well situated, close to the market, and on the main route for all the villagers coming in. I worked there for six months, drawing very little money for my own use in order to increase the capital.

We began to feel more settled in Tarsus. Everyone had work, and soon we began buying furniture for our house and living quite comfortably. Then, in November 1921, the French officers declared that the French army would be withdrawing from Cilicia. This came as a great shock to the Armenians. Now we would be obliged to uproot again and leave with the retiring French. To stay behind with the Turks would be asking for death. Our neighbour at the shop was a Turk. While the French army was in Tarsus he had never said anything to us, but after the French had announced their intention to leave he began to speak out against the Armenians. I was speaking to him once, and I mentioned that anybody who had resisted the Turks in the past was about to get their punishment!" and he replied, "We all know who has done what, and where they are now." Then he added "Aren't you the corporal who was at the garden of Koer Oghlan?"

It was time for Armenians to sell up their household items, furniture and any business supplies, but it was impossible to find buyers for anything. Everyone knew that we would soon be forced to move on, and our goods would remain behind for anybody to help themselves. At the first opportunity, Armenians began to leave. First the wealthy moved out, going to Mersin and from there to Cyprus, which was a British colony.

But to land in Cyprus cost £25 per person, and many could not afford that. My uncle Mr Hampartsum Pambakian took his family and went to Cyprus. My brother Yervant moved with his in-laws to Antioch, which was where they came from. We three remaining brothers and our aunt went to Mersin, but we had no money to go on to Syria. There were no boats from Mersin.

Messina was soon full of refugees from Adana, Tarsus, and other places. Some families found houses; others settled in churchyards or in the streets. Soon the streets were filled with horses, and baggage, heaped up in large piles. They were terrible days.

Soon we were told that there were boats for Smyrna, Greece and Egypt, but not for Syria. Those wishing to travel should purchase a visa. We all got visas for Greece. The Greek consulate made a pretty penny out of that announcement, although it didn't do anybody else any good. Two or three days later we heard that another country would open its doors, and we were advised to get visas for that country. So it went on, until all the consulates had lined their pockets and we Armenians were rich in visas. Still we waited uneasily for a boat to take us anywhere.

At last, the period of French control came to an end. Turkish soldiers came down to Mersin. The French handed over every office to the Turks except the customs office. It was dangerous for any Armenian to be in the streets at night. The Turks used to beat us, and some Armenians completely disappeared. All this while the French were still in Mersin. At last, in November 1921, a French boat came. About 1,500 names were registered, with no passport or visa. The next day we all went to the boat. Two other families from Adana were travelling with us, and we helped each other get on to the boat. The next morning the boat arrived in the Beirut harbour and we were taken to land in small boats.

Life in Beirut

We three families from Adana landed in Beirut together. I saw French army lorries full of Armenian refugees. They were being taken to Karantina. Immediately I led the families of my party towards them. Just as I was about to get onto the lorry a hand touched my back. I turned and saw a French captain. I saluted him, and he asked me to stay and help him organise the refugees who were coming out of the boat. "Let the men walk," he said, "and put the women and children into the lorries." I stayed until evening helping with the general organisation, and finally left myself in the last lorry. Fortunately when we arrived in Karantina I found the boys and Auntie. It was cold there, and we huddled together on one blanket and covered ourselves with the other.

The next day officials came from Karantina to record our names. They were Arabs. Those who knew Arabic, like myself, began to help them with translation. They asked everyone which country they were from, their occupation, where they were going, and how many were in their family.

Then a group of us under a French sergeant went to the river-side together and pitched tents there. The French officer announced that those who were ready and willing to obey the discipline of the camp could go to the tents. The rest could leave Karantina and go where they pleased. Many went, but ten to 15 families were willing to obey camp rules and stay in the tents near Karantina. Our party did neither. One of us found work as a cook, and thanks to him we were all allowed to stay in a room near the kitchen. But the next day more refugees arrived, and we were forced to leave our room. We decided to submit to the rules of the camp and live in the tents. I was used to the discipline of the army, and I didn't think camp rules would be too difficult for me. However, by this time, there was no opportunity to go down to the tents. We came out of Karantina and waited on the road for a while, until we saw the captain on his way down to the tents. We stopped him, and told him that we had been detained in Karantina to work in the kitchen, but now we would like to go down to the tents. So my brothers, aunt and I got a lift to the tents in the captain's car! The sergeant whom I had helped pitch the tents was also there. They gave us a tent.

The others had already been receiving rations: tea, sugar, bread, meat, and other things. The sergeant in charge gave me plenty of everything. After three days we were told to go and get our baggage. The customs was overflowing with bags and cases, all piled high in huge towers. The porters at the harbour took us in, and in all that mass of luggage I managed to find our belongings. There were people waiting outside for permission to go in, even trying to bribe the porters, but permission was denied to some for a long time, and they were forced to sleep there in the open waiting to be allowed in to collect their goods.

Army lorries came and we loaded them up. As they drove off to the station, we realised that we were being moved again, but we had no idea where to. That evening we left our tents and were taken down to the station. I asked the railway official where we were being taken, and he replied "Damascus". Many people wanted to go to Damascus, and were willing to give their last savings to be able to reach there, but were thwarted by their inability to get their baggage out of customs. And we were being taken for free, at the expense of the government.

We travelled all night across the snow-topped mountains of Lebanon, and the following morning, on 25 December 1921, Christmas morning, we arrived in Damascus.

Life in Damascus

When we arrived in Damascus we were taken to Bab Sharki and put in a place that was rather like a stable, not far from the church. That night we slept on blankets on the floor. The next day we went back to the station for our baggage. I managed to hire a room with a friend, but I had to give my last *mijid* for it. We found a large bag of bulgar wheat and some other foodstuffs in the house, and these kept us going for the next three days. I managed to find some temporary work on the roads, and soon needed to replenish our dwindling supplies. I didn't even know the way to the market, so a friend went with me to show me. While I was looking around, I noticed a sewing machine. I stopped in front of it, looking, and the man invited me into his store. I told him I was looking for a tailor, and he pointed upstairs, and told me there were many tailors "up there". At first I hesitated, but I went up the stairs and entered a large room with a tailor's table in the centre. The tailor invited me in, and I asked him if he could give me any work. He gave me a piece of work to do. It was quite easy, and when I performed that task to his satisfaction, he told me I could come back the next day.

I worked there for the next nine months, receiving one *mijid* per day. We lived very well on this salary. My brothers Timoteos and Sarkis stopped working on the roads. Timoteos started doing door-to-door sales work, selling stockings, handkerchiefs and similar goods, and Sarkis started work in a coppersmith's shop. We were quite happy. Then my brother in Antioch wrote to me saying that if there was good tailor's work in Damascus, he would come there. I told him to come. Damascus was much bigger than Antioch and there was plenty of work. So he brought his family and they settled in Damascus. He and his father-in-law opened a merchant tailor's shop together, where they did good business. After progressing in my work, I also opened my own private tailor's shop.

During his time in Tarsus, my brother Timoteos had felt convicted of his sins. Knowing that only the Lord Jesus Christ could free him from his sins, he had accepted Christ's free redemption and been converted. Now in Damascus he felt the Spirit of God calling him to be an evangelist. He used to go to the most difficult towns in Syria and preach the Gospel among the Armenian communities.

My brother Sarkis was injured in his neck while working as a coppersmith. He had several operations, but his wound only became worse.

Then the Druze villages around Damascus rose up in rebellion against the French government. Many French soldiers were killed. The French retaliated by destroying the villages with bombs and cannon fire.

The next wave of rebellion broke out among the Arabs in Damascus. The French gathered their forces in the Citadel, and raided many Muslim quarters in the city, burning and destroying them. The Arabs counter attacked, breaking thousands of shop windows, robbing and looting. The whole city soon seemed to be on fire. Wherever the French saw any action, they bombed the entire district with planes. The city was in ruins. Nowhere was safe. At last Arab leaders went with the Greek bishop to the French General Sarrail, seeking a reconciliation. The general demanded that they bring 4,000 rifles and 100,000 pounds to pay for the damage within 24 hours. They signed the paper agreeing to this, and delivered what he demanded.

Many Armenians, me included, were sheltering in the British hospital during this time. News of the reconciliation soon reached us. Peace was re-established and we had nothing more to fear. Two Muslim *hojas* and two native Orthodox priests drove around the streets in a carriage announcing the peace to everyone in the town. Everybody was in the streets. I heard that my brother's shop had been robbed, and began to run towards my own shop, already fearing the worst. Sure enough, the place was bare; the table, sewing machine and every other piece of my scantily furnished shop had been taken.

I sank to the floor in despair. This last stroke was too much to bear. After four years of hard labour I had finally opened my shop, and settled down to what I hoped would be the start of normality and happiness. Just as I had begun to hope that my difficulties were behind me now and I could look forward to beginning my life once again, I'd lost it all and was pushed back to the starting line. How many more times would I be expected to rebuild my shattered existence, to pick myself up again from the last blow and start the climb again at the bottom, labouring in the honest expectation of better days to come, only to be knocked back by the worst again?

I no longer felt Damascus to be a safe place. Street robberies took place any time of the day or night. The government was too weak to establish order. The Arabs would come and demand money according to how much they thought you could pay. Those who refused to cooperate or failed to meet their demands found themselves being shipped away to the villages in the dead of night. I could write more about these terrible times, but my heart fails me. Let us move forward swiftly.

My uncle had written to me inviting me to join him in Cyprus, where he had found work for me in his business. At the time, my business had been progressing well and I had turned his offer down. Now, with my business ruined, I had little choice but to contact him again. I had been robbed of everything; could he send me the money for me to join him in Cyprus?

By way of reply I received a registered letter with a cheque for ten pounds and an entry visa for Cyprus. I made arrangements for Sarkis to stay with Timoteos in Tripoli. He could not travel to Cyprus because of his wound. I also sold what few possessions I owned for extra cash, and saying goodbye to Yervant in Damascus, I travelled down to Beirut with Sarkis, my aunt Miss Senem Pambakian and my niece Azniv. From Beirut Sarkis went on to

Timoteos in Tripoli and Azniv travelled on to Aleppo, where my uncle was living. Azniv was engaged to his son. They were married soon after her arrival.

I left Damascus with mixed emotions. It was a beautiful city, abundant in fruits and vegetables, prosperous and pleasant. The Abana and Pharpar rivers flowed through the city, their banks surrounded by lush green fields and gardens. General Naaman, the leper, had boasted of these rivers, comparing them to the muddy waters of Jordan (2 Kings 5:12). Beautiful gardens and orchards spread for miles and miles around this city, making the whole place like a Garden of Eden. The Arabs call it "*Shami Sharif*", "Glorious Damascus", or "*Evvel Sham, Akhir Sham*", meaning "Damascus, the First and Last". It is mentioned as early as the times of Abraham, who passed through these plains grazing his cattle on the way from Ur of the Chaldees to the Promised Land. His faithful servant Eleazar was from Damascus.

We Armenians had all become fond of Damascus. We had settled down and begun good businesses. But when trouble came, we were once more scattered, as each fled one way or another seeking safety.

Many went from Damascus to Beirut, where a large refugee population was building up, and accommodation was difficult to find. On our arrival we found accommodation in a hostel, where we stayed for three days. Azniv and Sarkis continued their onward journeys, and Auntie and I were left together. We went to the Armenian camp to stay with a friend. I tried to get a passport, but was told that as I was from Damascus I would have to go back there to get my passport. It would be almost impossible to return. As it was, we had arrived in an armoured train, and Arabs were cutting the railway lines.

So we came up with another plan. I went to see a Mr Karamanlian, who had been our neighbour in Marash. He was working now preparing passports, and was able to help me greatly.

All I needed to do was prove that I had been in Beirut for eight months. We went to the Arab *mukhtar* and paid him for a certificate signed by two witnesses stating that I had been in Beirut for eight months. This certificate I took to the assistant commissioner of the refugee camp, who also signed and stamped it. Once I was an official refugee of the Armenian Camp in Beirut it was easy to get a passport. It took about a month. Early in the morning of 31 March 1926 I arrived in Cyprus, with my aunt, and our friends, the family of Mr Sarkis Sallakian.

Chapter 8

A Home in Cyprus

Life in Cyprus

We came to port at Famagusta harbour in Cyprus, and from there we took a car to Nicosia, via Larnaca. The journey took three hours. The driver took us to my uncle's shop, and from there to home. The next day he sent me to Amiandos, where there were asbestos mines. It was a large business, with many employees in the mines and factories.

My cousin Nazareth was running a grocery store with his partner. He owned the whole property There was a restaurant and coffee shop attached. I worked in this store as an assistant for almost six months. Then the mine work in Amiandos stopped and I came down to Nicosia, where I worked for about 18 months in a tailor's shop belonging to Hovsep Agha of Tarsus. After 18 months I returned to Amiandos to start my own business there.

My brother Sarkis's wound got better and he came to Cyprus and began working in the mining company as a tinsmith. I also came back to Nicosia for the winter season, and hired part of a shoemaker's shop, where I continued to work as a tailor.

One day our brother Timoteos unexpectedly came to Cyprus. It was a wonderful surprise to be reunited again on Cypriot soil. But my brother Yervant and his family left: for Sao Paulo, Brazil. He had children by now, a daughter, Victoria, and a son, Haroutune (Resurrection), who was named after our father. In America another son was born to him, and was named Albert.

My brother Timoteos was an avid preacher of the Gospel in Cyprus and many souls were saved under his ministry. The Spirit of the Lord had begun to move and work among us. During this time my brother Sarkis was also saved, bringing much joy to the family.

By this time my work had outgrown the corner of a shoe shop and I managed to find a suitable shop of my own. Business was going well. I made ready garments and sold them. My capital was only about four gold pounds, but I was steadily gaining the trust and confidence of the Nicosia merchants. I used to buy material on credit and sell it again, making a handsome profit.

My Conversion

Finally I also realised that I was a great sinner. My brother Timoteos used to witness to me continually about my soul, eternal life and eternal destruction, and the atonement of Christ. A few years before my conversion, the Lord had spoken to me in a dream. The dream had frightened me considerably, but I had not obeyed it. Now I could no longer refuse the invitation to come to Christ. I was afraid that if I rejected Jesus now I would never have another chance; no-one would ever speak to me again about my soul as my brother did. I decided to repent of my sin.

On 6 February 1931 I was awakened early in the morning. The Lord visited me again, and I could feel the burden of my sins weighing down on me like a crushing load. I was sharing a room with my brother, and I woke him up, saying, "Brother, get up! The Lord has answered your prayers; I can't wait any longer. I want to be saved."

We got up and prayed. I don't remember the exact words of my prayer, but it was something like this:

"Lord Jesus, you know I'm a sinner, and if I die in my sins I will go to hell. But you are merciful, and I know if I come to You, You will not turn me away. Therefore, this morning I come to you, with all my sins. Forgive my sins, and after this, give me strength to turn from my sins and help me. Amen."

That morning I felt as if a great burden was rolled from my heart. Praise the Lord: I was saved!

"There is therefore now no condemnation to them which are in Christ Jesus" (Romans 8:1). Neither is there salvation in any other: for there is none other name under heaven given among men, whereby we must be saved" (Acts 4:12).

Dear reader or friend, if you want to be saved there is only one way, and that way is Christ Jesus.

"But as many as received him, to them gave he power to become the sons of God, even to them that believe on his name" (John 1:12). "For God so loved the world that He gave His only begotten son, that whosoever believeth in Him should not perish, but have everlasting life" (John 3:16).

See how the Lord loves you! He is such a merciful saviour. He is willing to receive you also and forgive your sins. Don't neglect this great salvation. Don't be afraid.

God had a special purpose for saving my life when death and danger had threatened all around me: He desired to save my soul. The Lord has saved your life also from many dangers and from death. He has a special purpose for you, too: to save your soul from the second death and from hell. Don't reject Him. You may never be given another chance to be saved. One day it will be too late, and like the rich man you will open your eyes in the torments of hell.

Now I have my own drapery business. I praise the Lord continually for his blessings each day, both temporal and spiritual.

My brother Sarkis had an accident while working in the Amiandos Mining Company as a tinsmith. He became scared and fell sick. We took him to several doctors, but they assured us it was nothing serious. He was simply weak, and needed rest and strength.

We gave him tonic medicines, and after a few months my brother Timoteos took him again to several doctors. One of these doctors told us that he was sick with T.B. Then Timoteos went to Beirut and arranged for Sarkis to stay in one of the sanatoriums there. We sent him, weeping. Timoteos came back to Cyprus, and Sarkis was moved to the Armenian National Sanatorium in Lebanon. He was there for ten years, continually witnessing to the other patients about Christ and about their souls. He was a blessing to many in that place. On 11 March 1941 he passed away to be with the Lord in glory. He will never come back to us, but we shall go to be with Him. Praise the Lord for this glorious hope.

While Sarkis was still in Cyprus Timoteos decided it was time I got married. I thought this over and set my heart on Miss Azniv Chorlian. We became engaged, and during that time Sarkis left for Beirut. Azniv was also saved and was teaching in the American Academy for Girls in Nicosia. Our engagement lasted from 14 March to 18 July 1931, when we were married. We are living a happy family life. My brother Timoteos then left for Beirut, where he also married. The Lord blessed us, and on 21 January 1934 gave us a son, whom we named Samuel. On 8 December 1935 the Lord gave us another son, and we called him Haroutune after my father, to keep my father's name alive. Our third son, Bedros (Peter) was given to us on 25 July 1940.

In June 1939 my brother Timoteos came with his wife and two sons to spend their summer holiday in Cyprus. I took them to one of the Cyprus summer resorts called Pedoulas. The water and air of this village is among the best. We shared a happy and joyful time together. From there, my brother went to Egypt as an evangelist, and from Egypt to Greece. He was to travel from there to Cyprus again, when we heard that the Germans had attacked Poland. Immediately my brother left Greece for Beirut. We also sent his family from Cyprus to join him in Beirut. In September 1939 the Second World War broke out.

Smpat and Azniv on their wedding day, 18 July, 1934

Smpat and Azniv with their three sons

Conclusion

The Armenian people have a strongly Christian identity. Many converted from Zoroastrianism to Christianity in the early centuries of the Christian era. Then in 301 AD the king of Armenia decided that his country was to be a Christian country, making it one of the earliest Christian nation-states.

Moving forward many centuries, we find the Armenians a despised and downtrodden minority under the Muslim Ottomans, whose empire was centred on Constantinople (Istanbul) in Turkey. Armenians were scattered all across the Ottoman Empire but particularly concentrated in Cilicia and eastern Anatolia. The Ottomans treated non-Muslims according to sharia regulations, which gave the non-Muslims an official second-class *dhimmi* status in comparison with Muslim citizens. This policy has been described as a system of "institutionalised prejudice". In the Ottoman context, it was part of the *millet* system that the Ottomans applied to various religious minorities within their empire; these minority communities were allowed a limited amount of power to regulate their own affairs through their own leaders but under overall Ottoman control.

Under pressure from the European powers, the Ottomans introduced the Tanzimat reforms in 1839 and 1856. These reforms were supposed to improve the situation of non-Muslims in the Ottoman Empire. The 1839 decree, which attributed the decline of the state to a failure to observe sharia properly, had little impact. The 1856 decree, however, made no mention of sharia; rather it specified various requirements completely contradictory to sharia, for example, that apostasy from Islam would not be punishable by death. Also in contrast to sharia, it stated that there should be equality between Muslims and non-Muslims in terms of military service (though non-Muslims could pay a tax in lieu), in taxation and in the administration of justice. It also stated that Muslims and non-Muslims should have equal access to schools and public employment.

The introduction of the reforms raised the expectations and aspirations of the Armenians and other minorities, who had previously endured their second-class status quietly and uncomplainingly. They now began to hope for something better and to press the government for protection from thefts, abductions, murders, fraud and punitive taxation. The government viewed this pressure as rebellion and responded harshly. The centuries-old status quo of dominant Muslims and subordinate non-Muslims – unjust but stable – vanished. The everyday discrimination and oppression endured by the Armenians grew worse in the second half of the 19th century, and they became increasingly restive. The 1878 Treaty of Berlin, after the third Russo-Turkish war, not only took from the Ottomans much of their European territory but also required more reforms and protection for the Armenians of eastern Anatolia. The Ottomans feared this was the thin end of the wedge, a prelude to future demands for Armenian autonomy or independence. The last straw for the Ottomans was when the Armenian nationalist political parties appealed to foreign powers for help, particularly to Britain. This appeal triggered nearly three decades of orchestrated, state-approved, anti-Armenian violence that began in 1894 and in which up to 1.5 million Armenians may have died out of a world Armenian population of four million.

The 1894-96 massacres were fomented by agents of the Ottoman sultan, who would incite the Turkish Muslims in a town to rise up against their Armenian Christian neighbours. Sultan Abdul Hamid II further encouraged the anti-Armenian violence by promoting a belief that Muslims could help themselves to the property of non-Muslims and kill them if they resisted. In addition, his agents would tell the Turks that the Armenians were plotting to attack them. This procedure was repeated in 13 large towns across the empire. It is estimated that 150,000 Armenians were killed during this period. When 8,000 Armenians were murdered in Urfa in December 1895, the young men were killed by the traditional ritual Islamic method for slaughtering animals. They were thrown on their backs, held by their hands and feet, and then their throats were slit while an Islamic prayer was recited.

Another series of massacres occurred in some 200 Cilician villages in 1909. They had a combination of causes, and it is not clear how much the government was responsible for them, especially given that the Committee of Union and Progress (CUP) in Istanbul was dealing with a counter-coup at the same time. The long-standing Muslim resentment of freedoms given to Christians was certainly one factor, doubtless exacerbated by very overt Armenian celebrations of these freedoms. But a significant new development was that many Armenians who had fled the massacres in the 1890s were by now settled in Cilicia; this created rumours that the Armenians wished to establish an independent nation there. Another factor could have been that the Armenians had been exercising their constitutional right to arm themselves, most likely prompted by the periodic murders of individual Armenians by Muslims. Estimates of the number of Armenians killed in 1909 range from 20,000 to 30,000, and several hundred other Christians were killed as well.

But the highest death toll of the Armenian genocide occurred during the First World War, peaking at an estimated 800,000 in the year 1915. The victims this time were mostly from eastern Anatolia.

The men and older boys were largely killed where they lived, and most of the rest died during deportation to various desert areas. Some succumbed to exposure, starvation or thirst, while others were murdered en route or at their destinations. This was the time when Elmas, whose story is recounted in the Appendix, saw her husband Garabed burned to death in a church and narrowly avoided being sent on the death march to Der El-Zor.

The primary perpetrators of this phase of the genocide were the leaders of the CUP, who were the ruling faction of the Ottoman government. The CUP had developed from the "Young Turks" opposition groups of the late 19th century and had seized power from the sultan in a coup in 1908. The nationalist CUP were concerned about the erosion of Ottoman territory and feared for the future of the empire, especially if the Armenians should seek independence. They suspected a military collaboration between the Armenians and the Russians, who had a history of supporting Christian independence movements in the Balkans. Unsurprisingly the massacres of 1894-96 had only made the Armenians keener to agitate for reform or autonomy, thus irking and alarming the Ottoman leadership still further. The same massacres had also set a precedent, "shaping the mind-set of state and victims alike".[1]

The massacres and deportations of the Armenians enabled the CUP to secure Anatolia as an ethnically purified core area of Turkish people. A *fatwa* issued in the early months of 1915 urged Ottoman Muslims to engage in jihad against non-Muslims and made clear that this should be understood to include physical warfare and fighting. Then the Interior Ministry ordered the arrest of Armenian political and community leaders, those suspected of any kind of rebellious attitude. Many were executed without proper trial.

---

1 Donald Bloxham, *The Great Game of Genocide: Imperialism, Nationalism and the Destruction of the Ottoman Armenians.* Oxford: Oxford University Press, 2005, p. 4.

Deportations began from Cilicia in March, the first deportees being sent to places where survival was challenging but not impossible. Large numbers of able-bodied Armenian men between the ages of 18 and 60 had already been disposed of by conscripting them the previous year as part of a general mobilisation in preparation for the First World War. The new Armenian recruits to the Ottoman army served for a while as unarmed labour and then were massacred by their Turkish officers and fellow soldiers. In late May the scale of deportation escalated dramatically, with the remaining Armenian population, mostly women and children, being sent to be settled in what the Ottoman authorities called "agricultural colonies". Their destinations were in fact barren areas without any provision of food, water or shelter, and it is clear that these deportees were not intended to survive. According to Ottoman records, 1.1 million were deported.

Walking barefoot over mountains and across the Der El-Zor desert with little or no food or water, the women and children were vulnerable to attack by their guards and by the local Kurds. They were soon robbed of anything they carried. Many were raped; many were killed. Many died of hunger, thirst and disease. The few remaining men were usually separated from the rest of the deportees and massacred. Hundreds of young women threw themselves into rivers or wells to drown; some drowned their babies too. Little girls were sold as wives to Kurdish ruffians. Some deportees were packed into cattle-trucks and sent to their doom by train. Others were kept alive for a while to work on extending the railway, women and children breaking stones and digging through the Taurus Mountains. Barely 20% of the deportees from this phase of deportation reached their destinations.

The remnant who stumbled past Aleppo towards Damascus found shelter in the villages between Aleppo and Homs. The Muslim Arabs living there welcomed in the persecuted Christian Armenians, even though they were different in both race and religion. That is the origin of the large Armenian minority in this area of modern Syria. But those sent towards the River Euphrates were not so fortunate. Though a few thousand found shelter in houses in the town of Al-Raqqa, most were herded into "concentration camps" in desert areas of Der El-Zor without any facilities. Those who did not perish from natural causes were soon slaughtered. It has been estimated that up to 150,000 Armenians were murdered in these concentration camps by Circassians, Chechens and Arabs, mainly in a series of massacres in the first half of 1916.

After the First World War, in which the Ottomans were defeated by the Allies, the nationalist leader Mustafa Kemal ("Atatürk") tried to re-establish Turkish control of Anatolia. In 1920 he launched an attack on the republic of Armenia, which had gained its independence from Russia in 1918. The Armenian army was no match for the Turkish forces, and Turkey soon "imposed a draconian peace on the republic, reducing its territory to the barren, land-locked lands possessed by the state today".[2] At the same time, tens of thousands of Armenians were leaving Cilicia as the Turkish nationalist forces drove out the French occupying force; many of these had only recently ventured back to Cilicia having fled during the First World War. Pressure was put on the few remaining Armenians in the Anatolian interior to force them out, and soon the only substantial Armenian presence that remained was in Istanbul, which found itself facing growing economic and political discrimination.

By 1923 an estimated pre-war population of two million Armenians scattered throughout the Ottoman Empire had been reduced to around 250,000, of whom 200,000 had converted to Islam. At least a million were dead (according to some estimates 1.5 million). The other quarter of a million or so had escaped to safe

---

2 Bloxham, *The Great Game of Genocide*, p. 5.

countries or had survived the deportation and were living in north-
ern Syria. Many Muslim Turks and Arabs disapproved of the genocide and refused to collaborate. Elmas's story testifies to the kindness and courage of several Muslims who helped her. However, all
those who did take part in the massacres were Muslims. Some
Armenians who were willing to convert to Islam were spared, but in
other cases the authorities deported the converts anyway, arguing
that they had converted only to try to save themselves. Smpat speaks
of how the Armenians believed they could have saved themselves
from being deported if they had been willing to embrace Islam but
none that he knew had chosen to do so. However, when his life was
overtly threatened he felt he had no option but to go through a conversion ceremony, not believing a word of what he was saying as he
recited the Muslim creed.

The majority of the converts were women and children brought
into Muslim households. From the middle of 1916 the killing
slowed down, but the forced Islamisation seems to have increased
amongst the surviving Armenians, including those who had been
left alive because of their useful professions, such as military doctors.
In 2011 the Kurdish mayor of Sur district launched free Armenian-
language classes at the municipality offices; they have proved very
popular, and it is thought that most of the students are the so-called
"hidden Armenians", descended from those who converted to Islam
to survive during the genocide.[3] Bloxham discusses the Armenian
genocide, comparing and contrasting it with contemporaneous
Ottoman persecution of Assyrians and Greeks, who were also
Christian:

> "The Armenian genocide was more systematic and thor-
> ough than the CUP's attack on the Assyrians. Collectively,

---

3 Amberin Zaman, "Turkey's Kurds Seek Forgiveness For 1915 Armenian Tragedy",
  Al-Monitor, 3 September 2013, www.al-monitor.com/pulse/originals/2013/09/turkey-
  kurds-seek-armenian-forgiveness.html (viewed 26 March 2015).

Armenian suffering was more intense, and the state intent more explicitly murderous, than was to be the case in either the post-war purge of 'ethnic Greeks' from Anatolia and the reciprocal purge of Muslims from Greek territory, or the prolonged Kemalist assault on the Kurds ... the Armenian genocide constitutes an unusually complete instance of communal obliteration."[4]

Can any lessons be learned from the horrors of the Armenian genocide? Turkey itself does not admit to the fact of the genocide, although several other nations have formally recognised the events of 1915 as such. However, it is heartening that a Kurdish mayor of Sur district in Turkey's south-eastern province Diyarbakir candidly regrets the part played by the Kurds in the terrible brutalities inflicted on the Armenians at that time and has apologised for it. "As Kurds we also bear responsibility for the suffering of the Armenians. We are sorry, and we need to prove it," said Abdullah Demirbas. Likewise, Hashim Hashimi, a Kurdish Muslim spiritual leader and former member of the Turkish parliament, has recently admitted, "Sadly, many imams were convincing people that if they killed an infidel they would find their place in heaven and be rewarded with beautiful girls."[5]

Perhaps the foremost lesson is that nothing has yet been learned. It is recounted that Hitler spoke on 22 August 1939 at his home in Obersalzberg of his intention of sending all Poles to their death, men, women and children. "Who, after all, speaks today of the annihilation of the Armenians?" he said.[6] A week later Germany invaded Poland. Whether or not Hitler did make this comment, it is undoubtedly true that little notice was taken by any other coun-

---

4 Bloxham, *The Great Game of Genocide*, p. 10.
5 Zaman, "Turkey's Kurds Seek Forgiveness For 1915 Armenian Tragedy".
6 Louis P. Lochner, *What About Germany?* New York, Dodd, Mead & Co., 1942, pp.1-4.

try of "the annihilation of the Armenians" and the lack of international outrage or response would certainly be an encouragement to anyone else planning to exterminate a people-group.

It cannot be claimed that the rest of the world was unaware of what was happening to the Armenians. Henry Morgenthau, the American ambassador to Turkey from 1913 to 1916, recorded in his memoir:

> ... the Kurds would sweep down from their mountain homes. Rushing up to the young girls, they would lift their veils and carry the pretty ones off to the hills. The would steal such children as pleased their fancy and mercilessly rob all the rest of the throng ... All the time that they were committing these depredations, the Kurds would freely massacre, and the screams of women and old men would add to the general horror.[7]

Morgenthau asked the American government to intervene but they did not. He tried in vain to use his own influence with those in power to stop what was happening. He drew international media attention to the genocide, but without effect. The only way he managed to help was by organising private relief efforts.

In the 21st century, we have seen an effective campaign of "religious cleansing" in Iraq, since the removal of Saddam Hussein, that has reduced the Christian community in ten years to just a quarter of its original strength. Many of those Iraqi Christians were Armenians. It may well be that readers of this book will live to see the complete eradication of the Christian presence in Iraq, a presence that dates from the first century AD. A parallel situation is now developing in Syria, since the Arab Spring uprising of 2011, and the

---

7 Henry Morgenthau, *Ambassador Morgenthau's Story*, Ann Arbor, Michigan: Gomidas Institute, 2000, pp. 209-210.

Church in that country is rapidly dwindling as Christians flee the threats and violence directed at them. The cruellest irony is that Syria had been the best place of sanctuary and refuge not only for the Armenians fleeing the 1915 genocide but also for the Iraqi Christians fleeing the anti-Christian violence in their homeland over the last decade. Just as for the Armenians a century ago, Western powers will not intervene and most of the international media show scant interest.

Where will the Christians of the Middle East go now? Since 1991 Armenians once again have their own free and independent homeland, Armenia, to which many are now fleeing from Syria. But what about the other Christians of the Middle East – ethnic Assyrians, Arabs and others? Those who have the means to migrate to the West are doing so in large numbers from Egypt, Palestine and even from Lebanon, which was until a few decades ago Christian-majority. At the same time, many nations are sub-dividing into their ethnic entities, for example former Yugoslavia. Within the Middle East, there is now an autonomous Kurdish region in Iraq, but what about the Christians? Is there a need for autonomous regions or even independent nation-states like Armenia for the other Christians of the Middle East?

Another lesson that should be learned is that great care and wisdom must be exercised when seeking to help oppressed non-Muslims, lest there be unintended negative consequences. Some scholars trace a chain reaction that started with Western pressure put on the Ottoman Empire to improve the treatment of their Armenian minority and ended a few decades later in a massive Ottoman campaign of violence and slaughter against the Armenians. According to this viewpoint, the West's good intentions tragically backfired and made the situation of the Armenians immeasurably worse than before; even more tragically, the West did nothing to intervene and stop the killing that they had inadvertently triggered.

But the possibility of this outcome could have been predicted from a knowledge of Islamic values and history. Islam places enormous value on honour and holds firmly to the belief that non-Muslims should be seen to be subordinate to Muslims. So any public advocacy by the non-Muslim West on behalf of a non-Muslim minority could be viewed as a source of shame and humiliation to the Muslim authorities. The lost honour of Islam would have to be restored by a decisive action to show its superiority.

Some Western commentators condemn Muslim reactions of this kind as immoral, which they certainly are according to the Judaeo-Christian values of the West. But the commentators need to understand that the Muslim authorities may believe themselves to be operating correctly, for Islam teaches that the good and honour of Islam itself are of far higher worth than the life and wellbeing of any individual, whether Muslim or non-Muslim. By this logic, it could be right and proper to kill an individual, or even a whole people-group, if doing so would restore the honour and prestige of the Muslim authorities and hence of Islam itself. This mind-set has been imbued in Muslims over generations so that, even though some of the Ottoman leaders of the early 20th century may have been atheists, they would still have been largely guided by this teaching. They may well have thought the primacy of religion over people was a universally accepted norm across the whole planet. I am reminded of the recent comments of a British scholar enthusing about the 2600-year-old Cyrus cylinder, discovered in the ruins of ancient Babylon and now hailed as the first known statement of human rights. These rights, said the scholar, are universal human values about which all would agree. The values to which he referred are so deeply embedded in the Western psyche that he could not imagine any humans could think differently, and yet billions do.

A Message for Today

The story, which Smpat Chorbadjian has so vividly related, graphically illustrates the plight of individual Christians who find themselves caught up in major global conflicts, and in clashes between the value systems of Islam and Christianity. He and his family were ordinary people who sought – as most of us do – to lead industrious, normal lives in peace and harmony with their neighbours, until persecution and a calculated extermination programme rendered such aspirations impossible. Throughout the long period of dispossession and exile which Smpat recalls, it is clear that he held on with courage, resourcefulness and determination. Ultimately he came to a personal faith and trust in the gracious, merciful Lord who, he believed, had worked to deliver him, and to preserve him through all his troubles.

Patrick Sookhdeo PhD, DD
March 2015

Glossary of Unfamiliar Terms

agil – Arab head dress, usually a square of cotton secured with a head band

ayran – sour milk

bamya – okra

batljan – aubergine

brigands – insurgent fighters or bandits

'faddal' – 'help yourself'

hamam – Turkish bath

hojas – Muslim priests

jandarma – Turkish soldiers

kaymakam – governor

mashleh – outer garment, cloak

melengach – likely to be melengic trees, also known as pistachio trees

metelik – small coin of very little value

mijid – coin small in value

muhajir – refugee, emigrant

mukhtar – village or local chief

oke – a unit of weight equal to roughly 1.25 kg.

piastres – a unit of Egyptian currency

rouplees – coins

Saray (the) – palace, and may possibly include the settlement around the palace; official, government building

sharif – title given to an Arab ruler; noble or high born person

tekke – abbey

Vartabad – Chief Priest

yavshan – sweet-smelling hay

Appendix

The Testimony of Elmas

Two of Smpat's sons married two sisters, who shared the story of what happened to their grandmother Elmas. We wish to thank the family for giving us permission to make this account available here. It offers further illustration of the appalling suffering endured by Armenian Christians in the period of the genocide. It also shows the courage and faith of Elmas herself, and her experience of God's deliverance and mercy.

Elmas was a young Armenian woman living in the Turkish village of Habousi in 1914 with her son Mardiros, who was almost two years old. Her husband Garabed had gone to America to seek his fortune, and after a long time she received a letter from him saying that his work at the factory was thriving and that she and little Mardiros should travel out to join him. But Elmas's mother-in-law forbade her from going, explaining that the long sea journey of many weeks was not safe for a young woman and child to take on their own. With tears streaming from her eyes, Elmas wrote to Garabed explaining why she could not come and join him.

When the letter finally reached Garabed in Massachusetts, he decided to travel to Turkey himself and bring his wife and son back to America with him. He arrived and made his way to Habousi, getting to the village after dark one night. As he approached the house, he began to sing Elmas's favourite song *Es inch zouloum ashghar*. Elmas was amazed to be woken by what sounded like the voice of her dear husband singing the much loved tune, and thought she must be dreaming, as she knew he was thousands of miles away in America. But the voice drew nearer and nearer, and, hardly daring to believe it could be him, she went to the door and called his name. What joy she had to be reunited with him!

Within a few weeks, before Elmas and Garabed had said their goodbyes and completed their arrangements to travel to America, Garabed was arrested by the Turkish military, along with many other Armenian young men. They were imprisoned in the Armenian Gregorian church in Habousi. Elmas, who was now pregnant, visited Garabed every day to bring food, though he pleaded with her not to do so because of the danger she was putting herself in.

After some months, the Armenian men were told by their captors, "Convert to Islam and you will be safe."

"We are Christians!" the Armenians shouted.

In response the Turkish soldiers doused the church building with flammable liquid and set it on fire. Garabed and the other young men perished in the flames, which Elmas saw with her own eyes.

This incident was just one of many atrocities against the Armenian and Assyrian Christians of Turkey at that time. On one occasion Elmas saw a line of Armenian children being systematically beheaded by Turkish soldiers. Terrible thunder and lightning broke out, which the Turks relished as showing the approval of Allah for the killing of the Christian children. But when a bolt of lightning killed some of those doing the beheading, the rest of the soldiers were terrified, stopped the beheadings, and sent the remaining children away.

Some months later, the Turkish troops were moving street by street through Habousi, clearing the Armenian homes. On the same day, Elmas gave birth to a baby girl. The soldiers were about to start on Elmas's own street, but she was too weak from giving birth to try to get away Suddenly she was aware of a man with white hair, white beard and dressed all in white, who told her to get up and flee. She was amazed and knew her visitor was an angel. "But I can't," she explained, "I have only just had a baby, a few hours ago."

"I will help you," he replied, picking up the new-born baby. Somehow, he enabled Elmas, Mardiros and the baby to escape over the high walls that separated the rows of houses. Eventually, the angel brought them to a back street and into a house that was already empty and ransacked. He told them to wait there and keep absolutely quiet. He even handed Elmas a lump of sugar wrapped in a piece of cloth to give the baby to suck if she cried as Elmas had no milk to feed her. Then he gave Elmas the key to the house and disappeared. The Turkish troops were actively seeking her, aware that an Armenian woman had just given birth and therefore surely could not have got far, and eventually they came to the house. But though they entered and looked directly at her, Elmas realised they could not see her. God had blinded their eyes.

After some days, all those who had not been killed by the Turks emerged from their hiding places and met up with each other. There were very few of them. When Elmas's baby was eight days old she died, because Elmas had no food and could, therefore, produce no milk for her.

When the Turkish authorities had dealt with the Armenian men of military age, they turned their attention to the elderly, the women and the children, who were rounded up and told they were going to walk to a Der El-Zor, near Aleppo, where they could settle and live. All of them, even the pregnant women, were forced along the 350 miles route in the heat of the summer of 1915. Eventually, they realised that their promised destination was an empty desert region, with no settlements, no food and no water. Those who survived the journey to Der El-Zor were held in concentration centres, where many died of starvation and disease and up to 150,000 were deliberately slaughtered.

But this was all in the future, as Elmas, whose name was on the list to be deported, waited with a group of others who had to start the walk to Der El-Zor. As she stood, a Turkish *jandarma* came up to her, took her by the arm and drew her away from the rest of the women. "You are not going with that group," he said. "We have been ordered to kill those Armenian women, but your husband was a good friend of mine and I am not going to let you go with them." He hid her and Mardiros in a house and said he would be back in the evening. Sure enough, he did return, and said to Elmas, "Tell me where you want to go and I will take you."

Elmas said she would like to go back to her own home but the *jandarma* told her it was impossible as it would now be occupied by Turkish troops. "Garabed gave me something, which I have hidden in the rafters above the ceiling in one corner," she explained. "I would like to go and get it." The *jandarma* undertook to go himself and, being more senior than the troops occupying her home, he was able to retrieve the package from its hiding place and bring it to Elmas.

In the package were a lot of gold coins and a very large Armenian Bible. Elmas pressed the *jandarma* to accept the coins in return for saving her life. He refused, saying that she would need them for herself and her little boy. In the end she persuaded him to take just one coin.

Elmas was able to continue living in Turkey. But she was noticed by a Turkish village chief who saw how pretty she was and wanted to marry her. At first she refused, but he and his relatives beat her so brutally that eventually she had to consent. They began to make arrangements for a three-day wedding feast, which would have music all night, but Elmas was still thinking desperately how she could avoid the marriage. Garabed had brought with him from America a gramophone, and so Elmas suggested that someone should go to Habousi to bring it so that they could enjoy themselves more at the wedding celebration. Such a piece of equipment was unknown to many in Turkey at that time and they agreed to send someone to fetch the "music box". Elmas also suggested that it was not lawful to get married without bathing, so they agreed to take her to the communal *hamam* (Turkish bath).

Elmas packed some clothes and, taking three-year-old Mardiros with her, went into the *hamam*. While her guardian waited outside the main entrance, Elmas and Mardiros escaped from the building and made their way to the mountains. After walking for two nights, they reached a village where a good friend of Garabed lived, a notable Turk. Elmas told her story and he took her into his home. Meanwhile, the village chief who wanted to marry her was searching for her with a group of horsemen. Garabed's friend sheltered her for three days, as the search continued, and also for some time afterwards until the man who wanted to marry her gave up searching.

Then Elmas went back to her own village and began working as a housemaid for a very rich Turkish man. A couple of years later, Mardiros, now five years old, saw his mother crying and asked her why. She answered, "Because our boss will be moving permanently to Istanbul and wants to take you with him and raise you as his son." Mardiros said he would not go. Eventually, the day of the move came, and a beautiful cart arrived. The lady of the house seated herself in it, and her husband snatched Mardiros from his mother who was crying bitterly. He threw the little boy roughly into the cart, saying, "He will soon forget and stop crying." But Mardiros kept his promise about refusing to go. He began kicking and biting until the arms of the lady in the cart were bleeding. So she threw him out of the cart and abandoned the idea of taking him from his mother.

When Mardiros was about ten years old, he was taken to Lebanon with a group of orphans to be cared for in an orphanage run by a mission. Elmas had land to sell, so she sent him on ahead of her, intending to travel to Lebanon herself and to retrieve him from the orphanage once the business of the land was settled.

After Elmas had managed to sell the land she began her journey to Lebanon. She still had the gold coins from the parcel in the rafters. By means of those gold coins, Elmas was able gradually to make her way to Lebanon, giving a coin to each kind-hearted Turk along the way whom she asked to shelter and assist her. Then, when she reached the border, the Turks on duty there took away all the money that remained from the sale of the land. By the time she got to Lebanon she had nothing left apart from the Bible. Although it was as large as an A4 piece of paper and about 5cm thick, it had somehow survived innumerable searches by Turkish troops. Elmas and Mardiros (now eleven) were re-united, and settled in Lebanon together. Mardiros said that when he grew up he wanted to have twelve children because so many Armenians had died at the hands of the Turks.

Mardiros's ambition was not quite fulfilled in that he only had nine children, but these children were told many times by their grandmother Elmas the stories of her experiences as a young mother, the Lord's miraculous deliverance, and how she always thanked Him for everything that happened to her. Every day she read aloud from the same huge Bible that she had carried all the way from Turkey. One of her grandsons once asked her to read more quietly, but she refused, saying she wanted the words of the Bible to enter from their ears into their hearts. Likewise when she walked her grandchildren to and from school each day, she taught them Bible verses, giving sweets to those who could recite the verses word-perfect. One of the first passages she taught them was Psalm 23.

And what happened to that Bible? In 1979, during the Lebanese civil war (1975-1990), Mardiros, his wife Agavni and some of their children moved to Cyprus to escape the violence. (Elmas had died nine years earlier.) After a while news reached them that a rocket had landed on their home, leaving a gaping hole in the roof which was letting all the rain in. Mardiros returned to Lebanon to see the damage. He had the roof repaired but in the meantime everything in the home had been looted apart from the piano. The old Armenian Bible was gone. That was surely the greatest loss to the family. The Bible was wonderfully precious to them because of its place in their own family history. Furthermore it was an antique and – unusually for its time – was not only in the Armenian language but also in the Armenian script rather than Turkish script But the family hope and pray that the Bible will have been read by whoever took it and will have brought that person to know the Lord Jesus for himself.

Elmas's story could be multiplied many times over. Her home village of Habousi had been a close-knit community of some 3,000 Armenians but by the end of 1915 it was completely empty. All its inhabitants had been killed or forcibly removed or had fled. According to their descendants, the Turkish government afterwards purged all references to Habousi and its existence was officially forgotten. The remnants of its buildings were submerged in a lake created when the Turkish government built the Keban Dam, which was completed in 1974.[1] See the map for the location of the Keban Dam.

---

1 Compatriotic Union of Habousi, "Remembering a vanished Armenian village", 2011, www.myarmenianvillage.com (viewed 24 March 2015)